Sexual Violence:

A Bibliography of Theory, Research, and Intervention

E.J. Cho, BA

Leonard Snyder, MA, LPC

Herbert H. Laube, PhD, LMFT

This book is part of the series "MCNV Readings in Nonviolence".

Publisher:

Minnesota Center for Nonviolence

8609 Lyndale Avenue South

Minneapolis, MN 55420

admin@minnesotacenterfornonviolence.org

*Helping individuals and communities develop the resources and skills needed to live nonviolently in a complex world.*

This publication is supported by a blog maintained by the authors. Your comments are welcome. Please visit: mcnvspvbib.blogspot.com

# Contents

# Preface

We began this project with the modest but strongly felt purpose of providing counselors, therapists, social workers and other interested parties with basic information about sexual violence. We chose a brief annotated bibliography of current theory, research and intervention as the means to achieve that goal.

Like any other domain, the field of sexual violence is not without extant controversies. We chose not to speak directly to those controversies but to rely instead on the authors of the surveyed literature to make their cases. They are the experts in their fields. Readers of this bibliography can form their own judgements about what the authors have to say. We relied heavily on evidence-based sources to facilitate that end.

The scope of this project was limited. That was a purposeful decision. The subject area of sexual violence is too large for a single exhaustive treatment to be feasible. The content limitations, while perhaps disappointing to some readers, do not negate the usefulness of the bibliography. We believe it in fact has a high value in several ways. First, the emphasis on evidence-based literature raises the dialogue about sexual violence to a level above unsupported anecdotes. Experience is a capable teacher; experience backed by research even more so. Second, the reference lists in the selected articles themselves are a gold mine of further resources to be pursued by those readers who want more information.

We believe we have fulfilled our original purpose and we are proud of the results of our work. We are confident that readers will find this annotated bibliography a valued addition to their professional bookshelves.

One final note: The Violence against Women Act (VAWA) was passed in the U.S. House and Senate in 1994 and was signed into law in September of the same year. It has special meaning for us to release this work in the twenty-fifth anniversary month of VAWA.

E.J. Cho

Leonard Snyder

Herbert H. Laube

September 2019

# Introduction

*How the Bibliography was Constructed*

The authors began with a general idea that the bibliography must serve the needs of social workers, counselors, psychotherapists, physicians, nurses, educators and others who work with those whose lives are affected by sexual violence. It would include articles with a strong evidence base as a matter of best practice. Since the bibliography would be published by the Minnesota Center for Nonviolence, the mission of which is to help individuals and communities develop the skills and resources needed to live nonviolently, the selected articles would have a lot to say about methods for preventing or reducing violent behavior. Finally, the bibliography could not be all-encompassing and therefore careful article selection would be necessary for a useful result.

From there, one of the authors (E. J.) constructed many library searches and applied them to online databases, focusing on peer reviewed academic journals. E. J. refined the searches to develop a list of sources that would be the center of the annotated bibliography. Then E. J. drafted an annotation for each source. These two activities were the most time consuming and challenging part of the project and were the most significant factors in the success of the bibliography.

Next, another of the authors (Leonard) performed editorial functions. Multiple passes were made over the annotations to ensure a uniform style. Indexing software was used to create as an index that would improve accessibility to the bibliography. This index was manually edited to eliminate trivial keywords and produce a realistic level of summarization. An online tool was used to help ensure that the annotations met standards for fair use of copyrighted material; any areas of concern pointed to by the tool were addressed with minor revisions to the material. Some of the annotations contained citations for additional works; these works were added to the reference list. Some of the annotations made mention of various assessment tools or programs that were not themselves cited. Where it seemed appropriate, Leonard located sources that described the information in these uncited sources and added them to the supplemental resources list . Finally, Leonard drafted the preface and introduction and prepared the entire work for publication.

All three authors performed a final review of the complete document before publication.

Throughout the process, another of the authors (Herb) applied his decades of experience as a professor of education and mentor of graduate students to provide invaluable advice and reviews.

*APA Standard Adherence*

The Publication Manual of the American Psychological Association, 6th edition (American Psychological Association, 2010), was the general source of format standards used in constructing the bibliography. One significant change was applied to accommodate the needs of electronic book publication. Since e-book readers generally apply dynamic repagination, page numbers are not relevant for indexing purposes. Therefore, the sources were numbered, and the numbers are what appear in the index.

APA guidelines for reducing bias were followed in the construction of the annotations. The original language appearing in the titles of the articles reviewed was not changed, even in the cases where it might not meet the guidelines. Altering the original language would have complicated the reader's task in library searching and, equally important, would most likely have created a conflict with the copyrights of the various publishers.

Any reader of the bibliography who detects the use of biased language is strongly encouraged to call it to the attention of the authors. This will be invaluable in any potential future revisions of the bibliography.

*How to Access the Full Articles*

Readers who wish to access the annotated articles have several options. If you are currently a student, most schools can provide access to the databases that contain the articles reviewed. Many schools also provide access to library services for their alumni.

Public libraries may also be able to help you obtain the articles. A check of the Minneapolis, Minnesota Central Library web site, for example, states that many of the Ebsco ™ information databases are accessible through the library. The information specialists at your local library are generally very helpful at tracking down resources; it is well worth your time to ask them for assistance.

# Annotated Bibliography

1. Aberle, C. C., & Littlefield, R. P. (2001). Family functioning and sexual aggression in a sample of college men. *Journal of Interpersonal Violence, 16*(6), 565-579.
http://dx.doi.org/10.1177/088626001016006005

Based on the integrative etiological frames that identify the influence of family environments on the development of sexual aggression, the present study examines the influence of family-of-origin factors and rape-supportive attitudes on sexual aggression in sexually aggressive and non-aggressive college men. Participants (n = 76) were assessed on their family functioning (authoritarian parenting style, enmeshment, and conflict), rape myth acceptance, acceptance of interpersonal violence, negative sexual beliefs, and sexual aggression through self-report measures. The analyses of the data indicated that about 22% of the participants were sexually aggressive. The sexually aggressive participants did not exhibit more negative family functioning than non-aggressive participants, which was inconsistent with the hypotheses. The canonical correlation analysis found that the sum of rape-supportive attitude variables was correlated with the sum of family functioning variables although Pearson correlations found no significant relationships between the two groups of variables. Implications of the mixed-results and limitations of the present study are discussed.

Keywords: sexual aggression, family of origin, college male, rape myth acceptance

2. Acierno, R., Brady, K., Gray, M., Kilpatrick, D. G., Resnick, H., & Best, C. L. (2002). Psychopathology following interpersonal violence: A comparison of risk factors in older and younger adults. *Journal of Clinical Geropsychology, 8*(1), 13-23. http://dx.doi.org/10.1023/A:1013041907018

The present study examines the prevalence of risks factors (physical and sexual assault, poor health status, and recent exposure to trauma) and psychopathological consequences of exposure to the risk factors in younger women (18-35 years) and older women (55 years and older). A total of 549 older participants and 2,669 younger participants were recruited, and their experience of traumatic events, health status, and mental health symptoms were collected through structured telephone interviews. The results indicated that participants who experienced an assault or a recent trauma were more likely to have psychopathological symptoms. However, older participants were less likely to experience sexual and physical assault and to report PTSD symptoms and depression than younger participants. The multivariate analyses suggested that assault was associated with only one PTSD symptom in older adults (sexual assault with PTSD avoidance and physical assault with PTSD re-experiencing) while physical and sexual assault predicted all forms of PTSD symptoms and depression in younger participants. Low income predicted increased PTSD avoidance and depression only in younger women. Health status was not associated with emotional health, and recent trauma predicted only PTSD symptoms in both age groups. Implications of the age differences are discussed.

Keywords: assault, age difference, age related factors, depression, Post-Traumatic Stress Disorder

3. Acierno, R., Resnick, H. S., Flood, A., & Holmes, M. (2003). An acute post-rape intervention to prevent substance use and abuse. *Addictive Behaviors*, *28*(9), 1701-1715.
http://dx.doi.org/10.1016/j.addbeh.2003.08.043

The post-traumatic stress following victimization from a rape might increase the risk of substance use disorder, which might develop or strengthen as a coping strategy to endure the acute stress. Although these findings suggest that decreasing initial stress is helpful to minimize future psychopathological problems, the forensic examination of rape tends to magnify the acute stress experienced by the survivors. The present study develops and evaluates an acute post-rape, video intervention which aims to minimize initial anxiety during forensic examination and prevent substance abuse. A total of 124 participants were recruited and assigned to either video (intervention) condition or nonvideo (control) condition. Participants' lifetime, pre-rape, and recent use or abuse of substance, lifetime experience of sexual or physical abuse, and their minority status were collected. The analyses of the data suggested that the intervention was effective in reducing marijuana abuse six weeks after implementation. Although not statistically significant, the results also showed the trends of the video's effectiveness in reduction of alcohol and marijuana use among participants who reported previous use of the substances.

Keywords: psychopathology, rape, intervention, substance use and abuse

4. Ackard, D. M., & Neumark-Sztainer, D. (2002). Date violence and date rape among adolescents: Associations with disordered eating behaviors and psychological health. *Child Abuse & Neglect, 26*(5), 455-473. http://dx.doi.org/10.1016/S0145-2134(02)00322-8

Traumatic events during adolescents might pose a threat to development of a stable self-concept, including a positive body image. The present article, using a large sample of 81,247 participants, examines prevalence of dating violence and date rape in adolescents, their effects on disordered eating and psychological health, and potential associations with previous abuse experience and sociodemographic variables (age and race). Approximately 8.6% of girls and 6% of boys reported victimization from dating violence or rape. For both girls and boys, dating violence and rape were associated with higher risks of disordered eating habits: use of laxatives, vomiting, use of diet pills, skipping meals or fasting, and binge-eating. Participants who experienced both dating violence and/or rape also reported lower psychological health; they were more likely to report suicidal attempts and thoughts, lower emotional well-being, and lower self-esteem. These effects decreased, but still remained significant, after controlling for physical or sexual assault by an adult and sociodemographic variables. In addition, adolescents who reported dating violence were more likely to report other abuse by an adult compared to adolescents who did not report dating violence. Implications of the findings for future studies and the needs for early intervention are described.

Keywords: school-based concerns, dating violence, rape, eating disorder, suicidal attempt

5. Alink, L. R. A., Euser, S., Bakermans-Kranenburg, M. J., & van IJzendoorn, M. H. (2014). A challenging job: Physical and sexual violence towards group workers in youth residential care. *Child & Youth Care Forum*, *43*(2), 243-250. http://dx.doi.org/10.1007/s10566-013-9236-8

Group workers at youth residential facilities have been found to have higher risks of experience of violence. The present study investigates prevalence of physical and sexual victimization among youth care workers and potential influences of characteristics of group workers and types of care institution on the likelihood of victimization. The final sample included a total of 178 group workers. Participants were asked about their experience of verbal threat, physical threat, physical violence, and verbal and non-verbal sexual harassment perpetrated by the youth. The results suggested that 81% of the participants reported of at least one incidence of victimization. Verbal threats were the most common reported type of offense (78%); physical violence (37%) and sexual harassment (17%). Youth care workers at secure care were more likely to experience violence than those at group care. Workers at secure care were more likely to experience physical and verbal violence while workers in detention centers were more likely to experience sexual harassment. Also, workers with youth with mild intellectual disabilities were more likely to experience violence. In addition, younger participants were more likely to experience verbal threats than older participants were. Potential implications of the results and recommendations based on the findings are discussed.

Keywords: emerging issues: vulnerable populations, residential care, group worker, sexual harassment, physical violence

6. Allroggen, M., Rau, T., Ohlert, J., & Fegert, J. M. (2017). Lifetime prevalence and incidence of sexual victimization of adolescents in institutional care. *Child Abuse & Neglect, 66*, 23-30. http://dx.doi.org/10.1016/j.chiabu.2017.02.015

Children and adolescents living in residential care facilities are at higher risk of victimization from sexual violence. The present study examines prevalence of sexual victimization experience among adolescents in institutions (residential care facilities and boarding schools) and the natures of the violence in Germany. The results suggest that lifetime prevalence was 46.7% for girls and 8.0% for boys. Females were more likely to experience all types of sexual assault than males, and adolescents in residential care facilities were more likely to experience sexual assault with penetration than those in boarding schools but not other forms without penetration. About 5% of the participants reported their first severe sexual victimization occurred during their stay in the current institution; no differences were detected between adolescents living in boarding school and in residential cares. Most of the reported offenders were male. About 65% of the offenders were peers, but staffs also accounted for about 11% in offense. These findings suggest that lifetime prevalence of sexual violence is higher in adolescents living in institutions and that adolescents are at high risk of experience sexual victimization during their stay at the institutions.

Keywords: emerging issues: vulnerable populations, sexual violence, adolescents, residential care, boarding school

7. Angelone, D. J., Mitchell, D., & Grossi, L. (2015). Men's perceptions of an acquaintance rape: The role of relationship length, victim resistance, and gender role attitudes. *Journal of Interpersonal Violence*, *30*(13), 2278-2303. http://dx.doi.org/10.1177/0886260514552448

The present study examines assault-related and observer-related variables that might predict observers' perception of a sexual assault. The final sample included 284 male college students. The participants were shown vignettes about a male-to-female rape, with varying degrees of victim resistance and victim-perpetrator relationship. Their perception of the victim (culpability, trauma, credibility, and pleasure) and of the perpetrator (culpability, guilt, and sentencing) was assessed. Then, they were measured on their traditional gender role attitudes, hostile sexism, and benevolent sexism. Analyses of the data indicated that physical and verbal resistance of the victim, compared to no resistance, was associated with perception of higher victim credibility, perpetrator culpability, and perpetrator guilt, in addition to less victim culpability and lower victim pleasure. Participants' acceptance of gender role beliefs and hostile sexism was associated with perception of less victim credibility, victim trauma, perpetrator culpability, perpetrator guilt, and shorter suggested prison sentence, in addition to greater perceived victim pleasure and victim culpability. Relationship length and benevolent sexism were not related to attributions about victims. These findings might suggest that observers' gender attitudes are highly predictive of blame attribution in cases of sexual assaults. Implications of the findings are discussed.

Keywords: gender factors, gender attitudes, rape, victim resistance, victim-perpetrator relationship

8. Arata, C. M., & Lindman, L. (2002). Marriage, child abuse, and sexual revictimization. *Journal of Interpersonal Violence*, *17*(9), 953-971. http://dx.doi.org/10.1177/0886260502017009003

Although child sexual abuse has been well established as a risk factor for additional sexual victimization in later life, identification of its mediating variables (e.g. behavioral or personal variables) has been less successful. The present article investigates different types of child abuse, family functioning, dating behavior, and personality variables as risk factors for sexual revictimization in adolescent or young adult women. Experience of child physical abuse, child sexual abuse, the number of sexual or dating partners, being married, and younger age was found to be correlated with increased risk of sexual revictimization. Child physical abuse was found to have greater contributions to sexual revictimization than child sexual abuse. Self-silencing behavior and family-of-origin factors were not related to sexual revictimization, contrary to the hypotheses. Separate analysis for married versus single women found different predictors for sexual revictimization; for example, child sexual abuse predicted sexual revictimization only in married women. Based on the findings, future studies might address the influence of marital status of women on sexual revictimization and employ more refined assessment tools to measure child abuse and sexual victimization.

Keywords: family of origin, sexual victimization, child abuse, dating violence, personality variables

9. Ashmore, T., Spangaro, J., & McNamara, L. (2015). 'I was raped by Santa Claus': Responding to disclosures of sexual assault in mental health inpatient facilities. *International Journal of Mental Health Nursing*, 24(2), 139-148. http://dx.doi.org/10.1111/inm.12114

Based on the trauma-informed care model, the present article introduces a frame for understanding and responding to disclosure of sexual violence which occurred to institutionalized people with severe mental illnesses, who might be at higher risk of sexual victimization but unable to provide a coherent accounts of assault due to their psychosis or traumatic states. The present study introduces a frame consisting of five disclosure types and case examples and practice implications for each type: (1) recent sexual assault, (2) triggered disclosure of past sexual assault, (3) repetitive disclosure of past sexual assault, (4) delusional disclosure, and (5) intentional false disclosure. Regardless of disclosure type, an account might be plausible or not; however, persuasiveness of an account does not always reflect its veracity. All disclosures need to be regarded seriously and responded appropriately, through both therapeutic and investigative approaches. Initial response to a disclosure of sexual harassment should be thorough investigation of the account to identify disclosure type, validation of the individual's account, and assessment of trauma. Re-establishing safety and care-planning to respond to distress would be followed. After appropriate responses, analysis of risk factors and preventive actions should be taken.

Keywords: emerging issues: vulnerable populations, sexual violence, inpatient facilities, trauma, disclosure

10. Baker, M. W., Sugar, N. F., & Eckert, L. O. (2009). Sexual assault of older women: Risk and vulnerability by living arrangement. *Sexuality Research & Social Policy: A Journal of the NSRC, 6*(4), 79-87. http://dx.doi.org/10.1525/srsp.2009.6.4.79

The present study explores how vulnerabilities in the older women population interact with risks present in different living arrangements to influence sexual assault characteristics. Data included a total of 198 cases involving women aged 50 or older, which were collected from urban sexual assault center. Victim characteristics, suspected offender characteristics, assault characteristics, and predictor variables including where assault occurred were analyzed. The results suggest that about three quarters of the victims were found to have some form of disability. Differences in victim ages and consciousness impairments at the onset of offense were detected based on victims' living arrangements. Perpetrator-victim relationship also differed. Service providers were found to be a major perpetrator type for assault occurred in institutional settings, and in unknown. For cases in domestic and institutional settings, acquaintances and friends accounted for almost half of the perpetration. Women in domestic and unknown settings were more likely to experience coercion during assault and acute physical injury while women in institutional settings were more likely to report abuse of authority but no weapon use. Implications of the findings for practice, policy, and future research are discussed.

Keywords: age related factors, sexual assault, older adults, living arrangements

11. Bindesbøl Holm Johansen, K., Pedersen, B. M., & Tjørnhøj-Thomsen, T. (2018). Visual gossiping: Non-consensual 'nude' sharing among young people in Denmark. *Culture, Health & Sexuality*. Advance online publication.
http://dx.doi.org/10.1080/13691058.2018.1534140

The prevalence, gender dynamics, and consequences of sexting and sharing of nude images have been investigated in quantitative and qualitative studies. Yet, their social dynamics still remain understudied. To address this gap, the present article frames non-consensual nude sharing as visual gossiping and investigates the social dynamics and implications of nonconsensual nude sharing among young people in Denmark. Focal group discussion and in-depth interviews with individuals were conducted. The analyses of the data suggested that nude-sharing acted as a bond for homosocial relationships. The act often represented a sign of trust in relationships. Gender differences in the functions and consequences of visual gossiping through nude sharing were also found. Participants discussed the negative impacts (mental and social) of being a victim of public nude sharing and moral judgments and blaming against the victims, usually harsher when the victims were girls. In addition, boys reported that having and sharing nude images of girls was symbols of their masculine status among male groups. They also expressed the paradox of acknowledging harm on the girls and wanting their nude images at the same time. These findings highlight the social and gendered dynamic in the act of non-consensual nude sharing.

Keywords: technology-involved issues, non-consensual nude sharing, visual gossiping, gender dynamic

12. Brown, S. L., & Forth, A. E. (1997). Psychopathy and sexual assault: Static risk factors, emotional precursors, and rapist subtypes. *Journal of Consulting and Clinical Psychology, 65*(5), 848-857.

Based on previous studies that investigated subtypes of violent offenders, the present article investigates the differences in static variables (e.g.

criminal history, victim injury, offender-victim relationship), crime motivations, and experience of dysphoric emotion among psychopathic and non-psychopathic sexual offenders. Sixty incarcerated sexual offenders were assessed and interviewed. The results showed that psychopaths were mostly classified as non-sadistic sexual or vindictive subtypes. Psychopathic participants experienced less intense negative emotions before the offense and were more likely to be motivated by opportunities than non-psychopathic counterparts. Psychopaths also had more extensive history of and earlier onsets of crimes than their non-psychopath counterparts, but not higher numbers of past sexual offenses or earlier age onsets of sexual offending. In addition, psychopaths were not more likely to offend sexually against strangers nor differed in amounts of victim injuries compared to non-psychopaths. These findings suggest possible differences in risk factors for sexual offense in psychopathic and non-psychopathic population as well as among different subtypes of rapists. Treatment programs need to consider heterogeneity of sexual offenders and offer tailored strategies to meet individual needs of each offender.

Keywords: typology of sexual offenders, psychopath, sexual offense, subtype

13. Burgess, A. W., & Morgenbesser, L. I. (2005). Sexual violence and seniors. *Brief Treatment and Crisis Intervention, 5*(2), 193-202. http://dx.doi.org/10.1093/brief-treatment/mhi016

Sexual violence against people over 60s has received little attention. The present article reviews cases of sexual violence against seniors to provide suggestions for clinical practice. Early detection of sexual violence might be interfered with victims' reluctance to report (especially their marital partner) and public disbelief in the elderly sexual abuse. Clinical practitioners who deliver interventions to the elderly victims would be able to develop trusting relationship with the elder and understand signs and symptoms of physical injury and emotional trauma. Rape trauma symptoms are commonly reported by the elderly victims. Individual counseling with the elderly might need to consider their diminished general health and cognitive functions as well as potential underreports of some symptoms. Group counseling and music therapy might be other therapy options. For the victims in nursing homes, a practitioner might employ expressive therapies, rather than talking therapies, develop a communication system using with the elder, and visit consistently. Interventions or family members of victims of sexual violence might also be helpful family members who suffer from guilt. Sexual assault can occur regardless of the victim/survivor's living situations: independent living, assisted living, or nursing home. Prevention programs might include public awareness and safety education for the elderly.

Keywords: age related factors, sexual violence, clinical treatment, intervention, older adult

14. Caron, S. L., & Carter, D. B. (1997). The relationships among sex role orientation, egalitarianism, attitudes toward sexuality, and attitudes toward violence against women. The *Journal*

*of Social Psychology, 137*(5), 568-587.
http://dx.doi.org/10.1080/00224549709595479

The present study investigates the associations among attitudes toward rape and rape myth, affective attitudes toward sexuality, attitudes toward gender-role egalitarianism, attitudes toward violence against women, and sex role orientation in a total of 618 college students. Participants took a questionnaire on their attitudes toward rape, sexual opinion, sex role egalitarianism, and personal attributes. As expected, several gender differences were detected. Male participants were more tolerant of rape than female participants, more likely to blame rape victims, more tolerant of rapists, and more likely to have a positive opinion about rape. Also, women were more egalitarian than men in the parental and marital roles while men were more egalitarian in the employment roles. Further analyses indicated that positive attitudes toward both heterosexuality and homosexuality and negative attitudes toward violence against women predicted intolerance of rape in men while negative attitudes about autosexuality predicted intolerance of rape in women. Egalitarian attitudes about parental and marital roles predicted intolerance of rape in both genders. Masculinity, positive attitudes toward heterosexuality, and positive attitudes toward heterosexuality were predictive of belief of rape as a form of masculinity. Attitudes toward pornography was not related to attitudes toward rape. Implications of these findings are discussed.

Keywords: gender factors, rape, egalitarianism, sexuality, sex role

15. Carr, J. L., & VanDeusen, K. M. (2002). The relationship between family of origin violence and dating violence in college men. *Journal of Interpersonal Violence, 17*(6), 630-646
http://dx.doi.org/10.1177/0886260502017006003

Prior studies have found two groups of risk factors for perpetration of violence in adult male population: early exposure to domestic violence and attitudes supporting of violence toward women. To further investigate these risk factors, the present study examines the relationships between witnessing interparental violence in family-of-origin, experience of childhood physical abuse, and perpetrating dating violence among college men. The participants were measured on the conflict-management tactics in their romantic relationship, between their parents, and between their parents and themselves, their sexual behaviors, hostile attitudes toward women, negative sexual beliefs, rape myth acceptance, and acceptance of violence toward women. Analyses of the data indicated that witnessing interparental violence was positively correlated with perpetration of physical dating violence while attitudes supportive of interpersonal violence was positively correlated with perpetration of sexual dating violence. Childhood victimization from violence did not predict perpetration of violence in the adulthood, which was inconsistent with previous findings. These findings suggest the effects of witness of violence during childhood and negative masculine attitudes on violence perpetration in a relationship. Limitations of the present study and implications of the findings are discussed.

Keywords: dating violence, family of origin, sexual violence, physical violence

16. Casey, E. A., Leek, C., Tolman, R. M., Allen, C. T., & Carlson, J. M. (2017). Getting men in the room: Perceptions of effective strategies to initiate men's involvement in gender-based violence prevention in a global sample. *Culture, Health & Sexuality, 19*(9), 979-995.
http://dx.doi.org/10.1080/13691058.2017.1281438

The present study investigates effectiveness of strategies to encourage male involvement into antiviolence programs from the perspective of men who organized or attended gender-based violence (GBV) prevention programs from different global regions. Potential 15 outreach strategies at individual level or community level were examined. A total of 346 participants took an online survey to rate effectiveness of and to make suggestions for the strategies. The results suggested that all strategies were generally regarded effective, but individual or social network-based approaches--men's support group, individual invitations from family members or friends, and initiating conversation with specific interest of the group—were deemed the most effective. Media or technology-based strategies and celebrity endorsement were deemed the least effective. Several regional differences were also detected. Participants in Asia rated public- or community-based strategies to be effective while participants in North America rated individualized invitations to be the most effective strategies. Community theatre and art events were considered less effective in North America and faith-based approach in Europe. Participants also acknowledged the tensions between male identity and engagement in prevention of GBV. Implications and limitations of the study are discussed.

Keywords: gendered violence prevention, male engagement, strategies, antiviolence

17. Casey, E. A., Tolman, R. M., Carlson, J., Allen, C. sT., & Storer, H. L. (2017). What motivates men's involvement in gender-based violence prevention? Latent class profiles and correlates in an international sample of men. *Men and Masculinities*, *20*(3), 294-316.

To investigate effective strategies for men's engagement in antiviolence, the present article examines men's motivation for involvement in gender-based violence (GBV) prevention programs and the relationship between initial motivations and program outcomes in a global sample of men who completed GBV prevention program. The most commonly reported reason for participation was concern for social justice issues (87%), followed by exposure to the issue of GBV through work, hearing a compelling story about domestic or sexual violence, and disclosure of violence from someone close to the participants. The least reported reason included past experience of using violence or being accused of using violence. Also, four profiles of motivation in the sample were detected: low personal connection, empathetic connection, violence exposed connection, and high personal and empathetic connection. These profiles did not differ in the sustainment of antiviolence attitudes and the scores on gender equality measures but showed some differences key ally variables such as recognition of male privilege, bystander variables, network connection with those supportive of antiviolence, supportive attitudes toward women, and behavioral change. Motivational differences by global regions were also identified. Implications of the findings are discussed.

Keywords: gender-based violence, antiviolence, male ally, motivation

18. Ceccato, V. (2014). The nature of rape places. *Journal of Environmental Psychology*, *40*, 97-107. http://dx.doi.org/10.1016/j.jenvp.2014.05.006

Based on routine activity and defensible space theory, the present study examines the spatial and temporal characteristics of urban landscape where outdoor rape took place in Stockholm, Sweden. Data were collected through police records and protocols and fieldwork on rape that reached court about distribution of rape places in the city. The results suggested that rape was likely to occur in areas that provided easy hiding (e.g. vegetation areas) and easy escape (through transportation). They also were likely to be secluded from their surroundings, with poor visibility and surveillance and often close to alcohol selling outlets. In addition, two-thirds of the rape cases occurred at evening and night, and more than a half during weekends and holidays. An investigation of context of rape indicated that victims and perpetrators often lived in nearby neighborhood, which might imply their shared spatial awareness. Different patterns about time and places were identified for rape cases in the inner-city areas and in the outer areas; this pattern reflects a similar distribution of locations with other crimes. The findings suggest both time and space might influence the potential likelihood of rape offense. Implications of the findings for future research and prevention strategies are discussed.

Keywords: rape, place, time, urban landscape

19. Chan, K. L. (2011). Correlates of childhood sexual abuse and intimate partner sexual victimization. *Partner Abuse*, 2(3), 365-381. http://dx.doi.org/10.1891/1946-6560.2.3.365

Individuals who have a history of child sexual abuse are at higher risks of sexual revictimization and intimate partner violence (IPV) during their adulthood. The present study examines the relationship between child sexual abuse (CSA) and experience of sexual IPV during adulthood among Asian college students through a cross-sectional design. Data were collected from a total of 3,388 Chinese university students on their victimization from sexual IPV, experience of CSA, experience of neglect during childhood, violent socialization, psychopathological symptoms, and demographic variables. The results indicated that about 28% of the participants experienced CSA with no gender difference in the prevalence. However, female students were more likely to experience victimization from sexual IPV than male students (24% versus 18%). Other forms of childhood adversities were also associated with increased risk of sexual IPV. Further analyses through multiphase logistic regression showed that CSA was the only childhood victimization independently associated with sexual IPV victimization. Gender, experience of having sex with current romantic partner, and current post traumatic stress symptoms also contributed to the risk of sexual IPV. Comparison of the findings with Western population and implications of the findings on prevention of revictimization in CSA survivors are discussed.

Keywords: family of origin, childhood sexual abuse, intimate partner violence, sexual violence

20. Cohen, L. J., & Galynker, I. I. (2002). Clinical features of pedophilia and implications for treatment. *Journal of Psychiatric Practice, 8*(5), 276-289. http://dx.doi.org/10.1097/00131746-200209000-00004

The present article starts by examining the terminology and clinical definitions of pedophilia and child molesters and describing difficulties of academic investigation of these population due to lies, cognitive distortions, and the sampling methods. Then, it reviews previous findings on characteristics of pedophilia (including an estimation of its prevalence, gender, age of onset, number of victims, frequency and type of act, violence, impulsivity, and lack of insight) and on features of victims (gender, age, and relationship between perpetrators and victims). Next, pedophilia subtypes (exclusive versus nonexclusive, incestuous versus nonincestuous, heterosexual versus homosexual or bisexual, true pedophilic versus nonpedophilic child molesters) and high clinical comorbidity with other psychopathologies (affective disorders, substance use, impulsivity, and other paraphilias as well as psychopathy, introversion lack of assertiveness, and cognitive distortions) are discussed. An etiological framework for pedophilia is described. Successful treatments for paraphilia would include accurate assessment, pharmacotherapy and cognitive-behavioral treatments. However, treatment of the population is difficult because of their high recidivism, drop-out, and noncompliance. This literature review suggests that pedophilia is a persistent, serious psychopathology, which is often complicated to treat. Effective treatments need to be long, integrative, and intensive.

Keywords: psychopathology, pedophilia, child molesters, etiology, treatment

21. Craig, L. A., Browne, K. D., Beech, A., & Stringer, I. (2006). Differences in personality and risk characteristics in sex, violent and general offenders. *Criminal Behaviour and Mental Health, 16*(3), 183-194. http://dx.doi.org/10.1002/cbm.618

Prior studies have detected differences between sexual offenders and non-sexual violent offenders in diverse characteristics such as personality, psychopathology, or selection of target. To further expand these findings, the present study investigates the differences in recidivism rates, personal history, and offense characteristics among sex, violent, and general offenders and assesses the validity of self-report measures on examination of personality variables in offender population. Data were gathered from a total of 139 male offenders (sexual = 80, violent = 43, and general = 16), including results on Special Hospitals Assessment of Personality and Socialization (SHAPS) and Sexual Violence Risk-20 (SVR-20). Analyses of the data indicated that violent offenders were more likely to have higher recidivism rates at a 10-year follow-up (violent:

74%, sexual: 36%, and general: 45%), to have greater psychopathologies, to offend against strangers, and to live chaotic lifestyles than sexual and general offenders. Meanwhile, sexual offenders were more likely to have a history of sexual convictions, to display negative attitudes toward treatment, and to minimize severity of their crimes. The SVR-20 was significantly correlated with reconviction rates. The findings support the similarities between sexual offenders and general offenders and the effectiveness of the self-report measures. Clinical implications are discussed.

Keywords: typology of sexual offenders,, personality, psychopathology, recidivism

22. Crockett, C., Cooper, B., & Brandl, B. (2018). Intersectional stigma and late-life intimate-partner and sexual violence: How social workers can bolster safety and healing for older survivors. *British Journal of Social Work*, *48*(4), 1000-1013. http://dx.doi.org/10.1093/bjsw/bcy049

The present article examines unique barriers to help-seeking in older women survivors of intimate partner violence (IPV) or sexual violence and provides recommendations for social work practice to support the older survivor population. Sexual violence in the older population has been less studied and recognized even in the #MeToo movement. The older, female survivors face intersection of stigmas about gender and age (sexism and ageism) and their cumulative negative effects. The discrimination against older survivors is also prevalent even among health services providers. These attitudinal barriers and intersections of stigma not only decrease the credibility of the violence the older women experience but also lead to invisibility of older victims/survivors. Next, practical barriers are discussed. Current IPV program are not suited for older survivors as they lack additional safety interventions to address older survivors' greater risks of difficulties. Furthermore, the limited program outreach and physical constraints of the program environments might have discouraged help-seeking in older women. Implicit biases in the faculties and paternalistic advocacy are also described. Finally, practical implications for social workers are listed: recognition of diversity of individual experiences of abuse, arrangement of peer-support groups, and preparation to confront and acknowledge own biases, etc.

Keywords: age related factors, intimate partner violence, sexual violence, social work, old adulthood

23. Daigneault, I., Vézina-Gagnon, P., Bourgeois, C., Esposito, T., & Hébert, M. (2017). Physical and mental health of children with substantiated sexual abuse: Gender comparisons from a matched-control cohort study. *Child Abuse & Neglect, 66*, 155-165. http://dx.doi.org/10.1016/j.chiabu.2017.02.038

Although it has been well-established that victims/survivors of sexual abuse suffer from physical and psychological problems, gender differences in short-term consequences of sexual abuse in children are not fully studied yet. To address this gap in research, the present study investigates gender differences in physical and mental health among sexually abused children. The sample was comprised of 882 sexually abused children and adolescents and of 882 matched children and adolescent from the general population. Their physical health and mental health, until five years post-abuse, were measured by all reports from the Ministry of Health's administrative databases. In the sexually abused children population, girls were 2.2 times more likely to report physical health problems than boys while boys were 2.3 times more likely to report severe mental health problems than girls. In the general population, girls were 1.8 times more likely to report physical health problems than boys. Annual report of severe mental health problems in the general population was less than 1%. These findings suggest for the needs to assess the health in children survivors of sexual abuse and provide appropriate health services and potential benefits of gendered approaches.

Keywords: gender factors, child sexual abuse, gender differences, health

24. Del Bove, G., Stermac, L., & Bainbridge, D. (2005). Comparisons of sexual assault among older and younger women. *Journal of Elder Abuse & Neglect, 17*(3), 1-18. http://dx.doi.org/10.1300/J084v17n03_01

Sexual assault of older victims/survivors have relatively little research attention; this is alarming since older victims tend not to report the assault and go undetected despite decreased resources to heal from the assault. The present study explores sexual assault experienced by older women by examining differences in characteristics of the assault among different age groups of female survivors: young (15-30 years old), mid-age (31-54 years old), and old (55 years and older). Data on client characteristics, service delivery characteristics, sexual assault characteristics, coercion, and physical injury were collected from a total of 212 females who experienced sexual assault from 1994 to 2002. The results indicated that older survivors were more likely to be living alone and possess vulnerabilities such as mental and cognitive issues than younger survivors. The sexual assault against older women was significantly likely to occur in the survivors' own home. No group difference in assailant-victim relationships, in types of assault, and physical injuries was found. Uses of physical violence and restraint were also equally prevalent in all age groups while use of weapons was more common in assault of younger women. Implications of the findings and suggestions for future research are discussed

Keywords: sexual assault, age related factors,, assault characteristics

25. Dellazizzo, L., Dugré, J. R., Berwald, M., Stafford, M.-C., Côté, G., Potvin, S., & Dumais, A. (2018). Distinct pathological profiles of inmates showcasing cluster B personality traits, mental disorders and substance use regarding violent behaviors. *Psychiatry Research, 260*, 371-378. http://dx.doi.org/10.1016/j.psychres.2017.12.006

Severe mental illness (SMI), substance use disorders (SUD) or Cluster B personality disorders (PD) have been studied as risk factors for elevated violent tendencies and criminality. Despite their high comorbidity, each variable might be associated with different violent behaviors. The present study attempts to identify offender subgroups in male inmates based on different combinations of these three risk factors. Six clusters of offender subgroups were identified, and two clusters represented sexual offenders: Cluster 2 and Cluster 6. Compared to non-sex offender clusters, offenders in these clusters were characterized by higher level of education, low prevalence of PDs and SUD and SMI, and fewest suicidal attempts. Cluster 2, "opportunistic sexual offenders," had the lowest prevalence of SMI but displayed antisocial lifestyle and SUDs, accompanying higher rates of drug-related offenses and other crimes. Cluster 6, "emotional-sexual offenders," had higher prevalence of mood disorder, SMI, and suicidal attempts compared to cluster 2, reflecting potential earlier experience of anger and frustration. Offenders in this cluster also displayed high levels of physical and sexual aggression. The clinical differences in combination of severe mental illness, substance use, and cluster B personality disorders among different clusters of offenders might guide development of individualized interventions for different offenders.

Keywords: severe mental illness, substance use disorder, cluster B personality disorder, Typology of sexual offenders

26. Diehl, C., Rees, J., & Bohner, G. (2018). Predicting sexual harassment from hostile sexism and short-term mating orientation: Relative strength of predictors depends on situational priming of power versus sex. *Violence Against Women, 24*(2), 123-143. http://dx.doi.org/10.1177/1077801216678092

Past studies suggest that different motives might underlie different types of sexual harassment—unwanted sexual attention and gender harassment. Based on previous findings, the present study examines whether implicit situational cues can increase motives of power versus sexuality and influence the effects of short-term mating orientation (STMO) and hostile sexism (HS) on sexual harassing behaviors in males. Participants were primed by different poster images to activate their sexual motivation or power motivation depending on their conditions. Their number of offensive personal remarks (unwanted sexual attention) or sexist jokes (gender harassment) sent to the female target were recorded and analyzed. Analyses of the data indicate that among participants who were primed with power motivation, HS was a significant predictor of gender harassment. Among participants who were primed with sexuality motivation, STMO was a significant predictor of unwanted sexual attention. Contrary to hypotheses, no association between HS and unwanted sexual attention was found. These findings support the causal relationship between motivation and sexual harassment and the associations among individual motivations, STMO, and HS. Implications of the findings are discussed.

Keywords: gender factors, hostile sexism, short-term mating orientation, sexual harassment, motivation

27. Draucker, C., & Martsolf, D. (2010). Life-course typology of adults who experienced sexual violence. *Journal of Interpersonal Violence, 25*(7), 1155-1182. http://dx.doi.org/10.1177/0886260509340537

More attention needs to be given to life course of survivors of sexual violence and to combination of multiple types and episodes of sexual violence to identify protective factors and investigate resilience. The present study investigates the typology of life course in adult female and male survivors from sexual violence. A total of 121 females and males were interviewed. A narrative, life-course approach was employed to describe the contents and forms of life-course narrative of individuals, and a person-oriented approach, a cross-case analysis, was employed to identify subgroups in the population. Six subgroups were identified: (a) life of turmoil, (b) life of struggles, (c) diminished life, (d) taking control of life, (e) finding peach in life, and (f) getting back to normal life. The contents and forms of the narratives and characteristics of the participants and the abuse were described. Based on the typology, potential demographic and environmental differences among the subgroups and their clinical implications are discussed.

Keywords: age related factors, sexual violence, narrative approach, typology, cross-case analysis

28. Draucker, C. B., Martsolf, D. S., Roller, C., Knapik, G. P., Ross, R., & Stidham, A. W. (2011). Healing from childhood sexual abuse: A theoretical model. *Journal of Child Sexual Abuse: Research, Treatment, & Program Innovations for Victims, Survivors, & Offenders, 20*(4), 435-466. http://dx.doi.org/10.1080/10538712.2011.588188

Childhood sexual abuse (CSA) is a prevalent problem that has serious, longitudinal consequences on individuals; however, survivors often achieve recovery and growth from the experience. Despite previous studies on coping strategies and healing of the survivors, a new approach is necessary to inform clinical practice for survivors. The present study aims to develop a theoretical model of adults' recovery from childhood sexual trauma. Data were collected through structured interviews with a community sample who experienced CSA about their healing and experience of other abuse. Interactive analyses of the data developed a four-stage model of healing that integrates five domains of functioning (Life patterns, parenting, disclosure, spirituality, and altruism) and contributing factors. Each stage—understanding the meaning of CSA, figuring out the meaning of CSA, tackling of the effects of CSA, and laying claim to one's life—is described with characteristics in each domain, contributing personal and contextual factors, and exemplars. The progress of healing was not always linear, and the model implies that healing is a dynamic, complex process. Implications of the findings for clinical practice are described.

Keywords: childhood sexual abuse, trauma, recovery, model

29. Drouin, M., Ross, J., & Tobin, E. (2015). Sexting: A new, digital vehicle for intimate partner aggression? *Computers in Human Behavior, 50*, 197-204. http://dx.doi.org/10.1016/j.chb.2015.04.001

The present article examines the relationship between sexting coercion and other forms of intimate partner violence and their impacts on mental health and trauma symptoms in a sample of 480 young adults. Roughly one in five participants reported engagement in unwanted sexting. Although there was no gender difference in experience of sexual coercion from a partner, females were more likely to participate in unwanted but consensual sexting. Participants were also more likely to experience less severe forms of sexting coercion (e.g. making them feel obliged) than more severe forms of coercion (e.g. physical coercion). Females were more likely to report experience of coercion tactics. Sexting was associated with sexual coercion and other forms of partner abuse. Rates of physical sex coercion were higher for women, but tactics for physical sexual coercion were similar to tactics for sexting. The negative impacts of sexting coercion on anxiety and depression were as strong as or often stronger than the impacts of traditional forms of partner aggression. Participants also reported their experience of sexting coercion to be more traumatic than experience of physical sexual coercion. For women, the traumatic effects of sexting coercion increased over time. Implications of the findings are discussed.

Keywords: technology-involved issues, sexting, sexual coercion, intimate partner violence, trauma

30. Dworkin, E. R., Menon, S. V., Bystrynski, J., & Allen, N. E. (2017). Sexual assault victimization and psychopathology: A review and meta-analysis. *Clinical Psychology Review*, 56, 65-81. http://dx.doi.org/10.1016/j.cpr.2017.06.002

The effects of sexual assault on development of PTSD and other psychological dysfunctions have been investigated during the last 40 years, yet unresolved questions remain regarding their relationships. The present article investigates whether a sexual assault is related particularly to PTSD or psychopathology in general and whether the relationships might be influenced by other factors (e.g. types of sexual assault, assessment quality, time since assault, or demographic variables) through a meta-analysis of studies from 1970 to 2014. The analysis suggests that history of sexual assault was associated with increased risk and severity of all psychopathologies. Among the disorders, PTSD and suicidality had the largest and robust effects. Larger effects were found for assaults involving stranger perpetrators, weapons, or physical injury, associated with more severe psychopathologies. Differences in operationalization of sexual assault (except for inclusion of attempted sexual assault), time elapsed since sexual assault, age at sexual assault, and demographic variables were not related to differences in effects. Limitations and implications of the study are discussed.

Keywords: sexual assault, psychopathology, PTSD

31. Eyssel, F., & Bohner, G. (2011). Schema effects of rape myth acceptance on judgments of guilt and blame in rape cases: The role of perceived entitlement to judge. *Journal of Interpersonal Violence, 26*(8), 1579-1605. http://dx.doi.org/10.1177/0886260510370593

The present study examines conditions and mechanisms that might facilitate the biasing effects of rape myth acceptance (RMA). In Experiment 1, participants were presented with a rape scenario and different amounts of case irrelevant information about the victim, the defendant, or both. When increased amounts of additional neutral information was given, especially about the defendant, participants with high RMA (versus participants with low RMA) were less likely to blame the defendant to be guilty and responsible. In Experiment 2, all participants were given the minimal amount of information about a rape case. However, participants in the social judgeability condition were made to believe that they were shown additional, subconscious information about the rape case although no actual information was presented. Compared to participants in the control condition, participants in social judgeability condition were more influenced by their level of RMA. A negative tendency between RMA and Need for Cognition was also found. These findings suggest that judgments about rape cases are influenced by individuals' level of RMA and that the biasing effects of RMA might be susceptible to one's sense of entitlement to judge.

Keywords: gender factors, schematic processing, rape myth acceptance, social judgeability

32. Feiring, C., Simon, V. A., Cleland, C. M., & Barrett, E. P. (2013). Potential pathways from stigmatization and externalizing behavior to anger and dating aggression in sexually abused youth. *Journal of Clinical Child and Adolescent Psychology, 42*(3), 309-322. http://dx.doi.org/10.1080/15374416.2012.736083

The present article investigates the pathways from externalizing behavioral problems and stigmatization (shame and self-blame) following experience of childhood sexual abuse (CSA) to later anger and aggression in romantic relationships in a longitudinal study. A total of 160 participants who experienced CSA were interviewed three times for data collection: at the time of discovery of abuse (T1), after one year (T2), and after six years (T2). At T1, abuse severity, externalizing symptoms, and stigmatization were measured. At T2, their externalizing symptoms and stigmatization were measured. At T3, their anger and dating aggression were measured. Analyses of the data showed that about 80% of the participants experienced some form of victimization and perpetration of dating aggression. Externalizing behavior at T1 was correlated with dating aggression at T3. Externalizing behavior problems at T2 and stigmatization at T1 and T2 were not correlated with dating aggression. Further analyses of the data through structural equation modeling indicated that externalizing behaviors predicted dating aggression, but not anger while stigmatization predicted dating aggression only through anger. Limitations and clinical implications of the findings are discussed.

Keywords: school-based concerns, childhood sexual abuse, externalizing behavioral problem, stigmatization, dating aggression

33. Foa, E. B., Hearst-Ikeda, D., & Perry, K. J. (1995). Evaluation of a brief cognitive-behavioral program for the prevention of chronic PTSD in recent assault victims. *Journal of Consulting and Clinical Psychology*, 63(6), 948-955.
http://dx.doi.org/10.1016/j.addbeh.2003.08.043

The article examined the effectiveness of a brief prevention program (BP) which aims to prevent development of PTSD symptoms in female survivors of recent sexual and non-sexual assaults. The program, offered through four weekly educational sessions, employed cognitive-behavioral techniques to teach stress-coping techniques (e.g. anxiety coping, emotional reliving) to 10 female assault survivors with PTSD symptoms. The effectiveness of the program was assessed twice, two months and five and a half months after the assault. The authors hypothesized that the participants who completed the program would display less PTSD and depression symptoms than female assault survivors who received only the assessments. The analyses suggested that participants in the BP condition showed greater improvements in PTSD symptoms at the first post-program assessment compared to participants in the control group. At the second assessment, participants in the BP condition still showed significantly fewer re-experiencing symptoms. The BP treatment was also effective in reducing depression overall. Despite the small sample sizes, the results imply usefulness of the cognitive-behavioral educations in relieving some mental health issues in female victim-survivors of recent assault.

Keywords: psychopathology, Post-Traumatic Stress Disorder, brief prevention program, assault survivor

34. Foshee, V. A., Bauman, K. E., Ennett, S. T., Suchindran, C., Benefield, T., & Linder, G. F. (2005). Assessing the effects of the dating violence

prevention program "Safe Dates" using random coefficient regression modeling. *Prevention Science*, 6(3), 245-258. http://dx.doi.org/10.1007/s11121-005-0007-0

The present study examines the longitudinal effectiveness of a dating violence prevention program, Safe Dates, on perpetration and victimization of physical, psychological, and sexual dating violence among adolescents, using the random coefficient regression modeling. Safe Dates program aims to change social norms and improve conflict management skills in participants to prevent the onset of dating violence (primary prevention) and to discontinue existing violent relationship (secondary prevention). The results suggest that adolescents in the program reported less perpetration of psychological, moderate physical, and sexual dating violence and less victimization of moderate physical violence three years after program participation. There was also a marginally significant effect on sexual violence victimization. These effects were significant for both primary and secondary preventions. The program did not reduce psychological victimization, severe physical victimization, or severe physical perpetration. Dating violence norms, gender-role norms, and awareness of community services were suggested as mediating factors. Implications for future programs for adolescent dating violence are described.

Keywords: school-based concerns, dating violence, sexual violence, prevention, adolescent

35. Foshee, V. A., Benefield, T. S., Ennett, S. T., Bauman, K. E., & Suchindran, C. (2004). Longitudinal

predictors of serious physical and sexual dating violence victimization during adolescence. *Preventive Medicine: An International Journal Devoted to Practice and Theory, 39*(5), 1007-1016. http://dx.doi.org/10.1016/j.ypmed.2004.04.014

The present article investigates longitudinal risk factors, at both individual level and environmental level, of persistent victimization from dating relationships which accompany serious physical and sexual dating violence. The results identified several risk factors for the onset of and chronic victimization from sexual and physical dating violence. The experience of intentional physical harm by an adult, low self-esteem, and involvement in a physical fight with a peer predicted the onset of victimization from physical dating violence in male adolescents. In addition to these variables, having a friend who has been a victim of dating violence, alcohol use, and being white, predicted chronic victimization in males. The experience of intentional physical harm by an adult predicted the onset of victimization from physical dating violence in female adolescents as well. In addition to that variable, living in a single-parent family predicted chronic victimization violence. Also, for females, the onset of victimization from sexual violence was associated with having a friend who has been the victim of dating violence and being depressed. In addition to those variables, gender stereotyping predicted chronic victimization from sexual dating violence. Implications of the findings for development of dating violence interventions are described.

Keywords: school-based concerns, dating violence victimization, adolescent, risk factors

36. Gannon, T. A., Collie, R. M., Ward, T., & Thakker, J. (2008). Rape: Psychopathology, theory and treatment. *Clinical Psychology Review*, *28*(6), 982-1008. http://dx.doi.org/10.1016/j.cpr.2008.02.005

The present article is a comprehensive review of past theories on different aspects of rape and rapists —definition, characteristics, theories of etiology, rehabilitation theories, treatment practices, and future directions—to guide clinical practitioners. Various characteristics of rapists including sociodemographic features, offending history, and psychopathological features, are compared with characteristics of general offender population and of child molester population. Different theories of etiology have examined the roles of diverse influences, such as psychopathology rooted in childhood, patriarchal values, evolutionary mechanisms, and cognitive functions on sexual aggression. Among these theories, social-cognitive theories and Integrated Theories of Sexual Offending have been supported for their clinical and research applicability. The self-regulation model, a theory of rehabilitation, has also been in use for several components in relapse prevention programs for sexual offenders. Studies on current treatment practices suggest that the most-used treatment approach for rapists is cognitive-behavioral approach based on multiple perspectives. Rapists, however, are treated along with child molesters, and specific treatment benefits for rapists have not been adequately assessed yet. Considering the similarities between rapists and general violent offenders, future interventions for rapists might benefit from applying effective approaches for general offenders. Implications and recommendations for future research and clinical programs are stated.

Keywords: psychopathology, rape, treatment, etiology

37. Gartner, R. E., & Sterzing, P. R. (2016). Gender microaggressions as a gateway to sexual harassment and sexual assault: Expanding the conceptualization of youth sexual violence. Affilia: *Journal of Women & Social Work, 31*(4), 491-503. http://dx.doi.org/10.1177/0886109916654732

Current conceptualization of youth sexual violence generally excludes continuous, less severe forms of aggression, or "gender microaggression," insulting remarks, assaults, or invalidations based on gender. The authors believe this exclusion is problematic since gender microaggression fosters an environment that normalizes sexual violence against females and less severe forms of violence might escalate to more severe forms of violence. First, through a feminist, ecological perspective, the literature on sexual assault, sexual harassment, and gender microaggression is reviewed to present the continuum of sexual violence and investigate the overlaps and differences in each form of violence. Despite its lowest severity, microaggression can also have mental health consequences on victims through its cumulative and continuous natures. Based on the review, a new, theoretically grounded model of youth sexual violence that addresses a full spectrum of violence, from low-severity to high-severity and from high-chronicity and to low-chronicity, in a continuum is introduced.

Gender microaggression is a distinctive form of youth sexual violence, which is highly chronic and maintains objectification of women and support male privilege. Last, Prevention approaches and research directions are discussed.

Keywords: gender factors, feminist perspective, gender microaggression, sexism, gender violence

38. Gokten, E. S., & Duman, N. S. (2016). Factors influencing the development of psychiatric disorders in the victims of sexual abuse: A study on Turkish children. *Children and Youth Services Review, 69*, 49-55. http://dx.doi.org/10.1016/j.childyouth.2016.07.022

The present article examines whether gender differences exist in characteristics of childhood sexual abuse (CSA) and mental health outcomes and whether CSA characteristics are related to psychopathological outcomes. A total of 482 cases of sexual abuse of children reported to the surveillance center in Turkey were investigated on demographic variables of the survivors and of abusers, characteristics of the abuse, and psychological outcomes for the survivors. In this sample, about 82% were girls and 18% were boys. The most commonly reported form of sexual abuse was sexual touching for girls and anal penetration for boys. About 42% of girls and 36% of boys experienced penetration. For cases involving both female and male survivors, most of the abusers were men. About 63% of the survivors (69% of female and 38% of male) reported at least one diagnosis of psychiatric disorder as a consequence of the sexual abuse. Multiple Regression analyses identified independent factors that predicted higher rates of diagnosis of psychiatric disorders: female gender, victimization from multiple incidents of abuse, experience of violence or force, and being the only victim in the incident. Comparison of current statistics with previous findings and implications of these findings are discussed.

Keywords: gender factors, child sexual abuse, psychiatric disorder, gender differences

39. Grove, L., Morrison-Beedy, D., Kirby, R., & Hess, J. (2018). The birds, bees, and special needs: Making evidence-based sex education accessible for adolescents with intellectual disabilities. *Sexuality and Disability*. Advance online publication.

Adolescents with intellectual disabilities (ID) have limited access to sex education despite their higher risk of sexual victimization and experience of unwanted pregnancy and sexually transmitted diseases as results. The present study assesses the HIPTeens curriculum, a brief, evidence-based sexual education intervention that can be modified and applied to adolescents with ID, through the Universal Design for Learning (UDL) curriculum check. The results indicated that the HIPTeens intervention included many components from UDL principles, especially regarding different means of action, expression, and engagement. Tables with UDL checkpoints and HIPTeens components are provided. The participant-centered intervention also provides various methods for interaction with the learning environment and expression of knowledge through physical activities, writings, multimedia interaction, and discussions. During the assessment, a few curricular gaps were detected, including a dearth of visual information and aids and limited options for information processing. To address these gaps, supplementary educational materials, including PowerPoint slides, handouts with graphics, and videos were established. Implications of the process and future recommendations are discussed.

*Keywords: emerging issues: vulnerable populations,* sex education, special needs, intellectual disabilities, Universal Design for Learning

40. Hald, G. M., Malamuth, N. M., & Yuen, C. (2010). Pornography and attitudes supporting violence against women: revisiting the relationship in nonexperimental studies. *Aggressive Behavior, 36*(1), 14-20. https://doi.org/10.1002/ab.20328

Although experimental studies have supported the relationships between pornography consumption and attitudes supporting violence against women, a meta-analysis by Allen et al. (1995) of nonexperimental studies failed to find a significant relationship between pornography contents and violent-supporting attitudes. To explore this inconsistency, the present study conducts another meta-analysis of nonexperimental studies and addresses questions and problems in Allen et al. (1995): a lack of fit of the studies in the analysis and statistical mistake. The final sample included a total of 2,309 participants in nine studies. The participants' attitudes supporting violence against women were measured through various scales: acceptance of interpersonal violence, adversarial sexual belief, rape myth acceptance, attitudes toward rape and sexual violence, and potential of rape or sexual aggression. The results found an overall significant relationship between pornography consumption and attitudes approving violence against women in the nonexperimental studies. This association was stronger for violent pornography than nonviolent pornography. These findings not only suggest that the results of nonexperimental studies are in fact consistent with results of experimental studies but also support the small but consistent effects of pornography on attitudes supporting violence against women.

Keywords: technology-involved issues, pornography consumption, violence against women, rape myth acceptance, sexual violence

41. Hayes, R. M., & Dragiewicz, M. (2018). Unsolicited dick pics: Erotica, exhibitionism or entitlement? *Women's Studies International Forum.* Advance online publication. http://dx.doi.org/10.1016/j.wsif.2018.07.001

Studies on technology-facilitated sexual violence mostly investigate non-consensual sharing of images of female, and less attention has been given to distribution of unsolicited dick pics targeting women. The authors argue that distribution of dick pics also deserves academic attention and research. The present article summarizes findings in different research areas to understand intentional distribution of dick images. The concept of continuum of sexual violence suggests that sexual violence might share the same motivations and causes with other normative behaviors. Thus, mainstream values that contribute to more severe and extreme forms of violence should be addressed. Based on this concept, entitlement, which has been found relevant to abuse of children and women, is reviewed regarding its contribution to men's distribution of dick pictures. Research of sexual entitlement and aggrieved entitlement suggests that the act is not only the representation of their belief of rights to have sex but also resistance to women's increasing power. Literature on image-based violence suggests that unsolicited dick pictures might be one form of online sexual harassment. The act is also compared with physical world offenses, such as "flashing" and public exposure of genital. Suggestions for future research are described.

Keywords: technology-involved issues, entitlement, sexual harassment, technology-facilitated sexual violence, image-based violence

42. Hedge, J. M., Sianko, N., & McDonell, J. R. (2017). Professional help-seeking for adolescent dating violence in the rural south: The role of social support and informal help-seeking. *Violence Against Women*, *23*(12), 1442-1461. http://dx.doi.org/10.1177/1077801216662342

Adolescents who experience dating violence might suffer from physical or psychological distress; however, rather than relying on professional or formal help, adolescents often turn to their friends and family for support or do not seek help at all. The present article examines the effects of perceived social support and informal help-seeking intentions on professional help-seeking intentions among adolescents experiencing dating violence. 589 adolescents from a rural, southern district were assessed on their intentions of help-seeking, sources of help, perceived social support, and experience of dating violence. The results suggest that the participants were somewhat likely to seek help for dating violence and more likely to seek informal help than professional help for overall dating violence. The willingness to seek help and the source of help differed by type of dating violence. For example, the participants were more likely to seek help for physical and sexual violence than for psychological violence. Also, informal help-seeking was found to mediate the association between perceived social support and professional help-seeking intentions. Implications of the results and suggestions for future prevention and intervention strategies are discussed.

Keywords: school-based concerns, adolescent, dating violence, help-seeking

43. Henry, N., & Powell, A. (2015). Embodied harms: Gender, shame, and technology-facilitated sexual violence. *Violence Against Women, 21*(6), 758-779. http://dx.doi.org/10.1177/1077801215576581

The present study examines the manifestation of retraditionalized gender hierarchies and inequalities in online space and conceptualizes technology-facilitated gender sexual violence and harassment (TFSV) as "embodied harms" against women. First, sociological and feminist perspectives on technology and gender structure are reviewed. Technologies have provided opportunities for overcoming physical constraints and attaining fluid identities; however, technologies might also contribute to retraditionalization of gender roles. Also, the characteristics of internet and online space, such as anonymity and ease of approaching many victims have created new forms of crimes and enabled traditional crimes to be perpetrated in new ways. Although harms in the virtual world can have real-world consequences, both physical and psychological, in individuals' lives, criminal laws are inadequate to respond to TFSV. Misrecognition of the TFSV results in failure to recognize its gendered nature and leads to difficulties in recognition of sexual harassment in online context. To accurately frame TFSV, it is crucial to acknowledge the new form of social shaming and understand objectification of female-body in TFSV in collectivist and individualistic terms. The authors conclude that the dualism of "real" and "virtual" contributes to failure to understand the embodied harms and argue for better understanding of the phenomena.

Keywords: technology-involved issues, technology-facilitated gender sexual violence, gendered violence, technology

44. Hillenbrand-Gunn, T. L., Heppner, M. J., Mauch, P. A., & Park, H.-J. (2010). Men as Allies: The efficacy of a high school rape prevention intervention. *Journal of Counseling & Development, 88*(1), 43-51. http://dx.doi.org/10.1002/j.1556-6678.2010.tb00149.x

A Men as Allies approach acknowledges the potentials of men as active participants in changing rape culture. Based on this perspective, social norms theory has been found promising in their application to rape prevention programs for targeting misconceptions about peer norms. The present study investigates the effectiveness of a high school rape prevention program, which integrates a "Men as allies" approach with accurate presentation of information about social norms, on participants' rape-supportive attitudes and behaviors and perception of peer norms. According to the data analyses, both male and female students who participated in the program exhibition significant reduction in rape-supportive attitudes; these effects were maintained at follow-up. However, male students' reported willingness to behavioral change was not maintained at the follow-up. In contrast, female students reported higher willingness to engage in rape-preventive behaviors after the program. As hypothesized, male students rated their peers to be more rape-supportive than the students actually rated themselves. After the intervention, both male and female students' rating of peers on rape-supportive attitudes significantly decreased. The findings support the applicability of social norms to rape prevention programs targeting adolescents. Strengths of the study and implications are discussed.

Keywords: school-based concerns, dating violence, rape-supportive attitudes, adolescent, rape prevention

45. Hunter, J. A. (1991). A comparison of the psychosocial maladjustment of adult males and females sexually molested as children. *Journal of Interpersonal Violence*, *6*(2), 205-217. http://dx.doi.org/10.1177/088626091006002005

The present article examines longitudinal effects of child sexual abuse on psychosocial adjustment and the roles of gender in adult survivors. Data were collected from 52 survivors and matched-number controls on their childhood development, family-of-origin histories, medical and psychiatry history, substance abuse, and victimization characteristic through interview and questionnaires. Both male and female survivors of child sexual abuse exhibited greater psychosocial dysfunctions (e.g. lower self-esteem, less satisfaction in romantic relationship, sexual maladjustment, and general emotional maladjustment) across multiple scales compared to the non-victimized control group. Investigation of victimization characteristics found several gender differences. Males were more likely to have an adolescent perpetrator while females were more likely to have an incestuous perpetrator (a father or a stepfather). Also, male survivors reported anxiety about identity and rumination while female survivors reported incongruences and disturbance to their body image. These findings support that survivors of child sexual abuse experience psychosocial maladjustments and gender of the survivors make differences. Further studies might continue to investigate short-term and long-term effects of sexual abuse and the effects on other variables.

Keywords: Gender factors, gender difference, child sexual abuse, psychosocial maladjustment

46. Jackson, S. M., Cram, F., & Seymour, F. W. (2000). Violence and sexual coercion in high school students' dating relationships. *Journal of Family Violence, 15*(1), 23-36. http://dx.doi.org/10.1023/A:1007545302987

The present study aims to extend knowledge about gender effects regarding adolescent dating violence by investigating different dimensions of violence in both male and female high school students. Through a questionnaire with open-ended and forced choices, participants' experience of different types of violence in dating relations (physical, emotional, and sexual), perceived reasons for the violence, emotional responses, help-seeking, relationship consequences, and demographics were assessed. The analyses suggest that a majority of the participants experienced at least one form of dating violence, and boys and girls reported similar rates of experience of all types of violence.

Experience of emotional violence (81.5% of girls; 76.3% of boys) and sexual coercion (76.9% of girls; 67.4% of boys) was higher than experience of physical violence (17.5% of girls; 13.3% of boys). Gender differences were apparent in emotional responses to violence, as male students reported more positive feelings than female students; these differences were largest in experience of sexual violence. Talking to someone else about violence was associated with positive outcomes but also with lower likelihood of discontinuing violence relationship. Female students were more likely to discuss violence with other people than male students. Suggestions for future research and implications for adolescent dating violence programs are discussed.

Keywords: school-based concerns, dating violence, sexual coercion, physical violence, emotional response

47. Jeary, K. (2005). Sexual abuse and sexual offending against elderly people: A focus on perpetrators and victims. *Journal of Forensic Psychiatry & Psychology, 16*(2), 328-343. http://dx.doi.org/10.1080/14789940500096115

The present study is a qualitative research project on a broad scope of sexual abuse against the elder. A total of 52 cases and 54 victims were examined through interviews thematically analyzed. Among the cases, different types of abuse are identified: sexual assault and homicide, rape or attempted rape, indecent assault, and sexual harassment. Age of perpetrator and of victim, offender-victim relationships, and assault places among the types of abuse are discussed.

Next, motivations of offenders are discussed. Self-absorption was referred by the majority of the perpetrators, and sexual inadequacy was also reported by many perpetrators. About one third of the sample reported their motivations to be sexual gratification. The desire for opportunities to yield power and control over others, especially female, and hostile attitudes toward women was also common. Frequency of reports of financial motivation was low in this sample. Furthermore, experience of childhood abuse among the offenders and comparison of characteristics of perpetrators of senior abuse and of minor abuse are discussed. Victims/survivors of older sexual assault report occurrence of excessive physical violence, humiliation, and use of weapons, during the assault, which resulted in severe physical injuries and long-term effects. Yet, the health care service offered to these victims was rarely recorded.

Keywords: age related factors, old adulthood, rape, sexual assault, offender characteristics

48. Kloess, J. A., Beech, A. R., & Harkins, L. (2014). Online child sexual exploitation: Prevalence, process, and offender characteristics. Trauma, Violence, & Abuse, 15(2), 126-139. http://dx.doi.org/10.1177/1524838013511543

The present review summarizes current understanding of on various factors of online sexual grooming and exploitation of children. Although reports of online sexual grooming among minor have increased, underreporting and children's inabilities to recognize sexual motives have been major challenges to estimate their prevalence. Also, legislation might not be able to fully respond to online sexual grooming due to absence of meeting between offenders and victims in online offenses. Literature on sexual grooming indicates that grooming acts as an onset of sexual abuse by preparing the target for compliance to the offender and confidentiality about engagement in sexual activities. Internet might facilitate overcoming of internal and external inhibiting factors by its playful, anonymous nature and ease of contacting with users and disguising oneself. Studies on online sexual grooming have identified different motivations, hunting behaviors, and strategies used by the perpetrators. The model of problematic internet use suggests that a combination of risk factors contribute to commitment of online sexual offense. Last, comparison of online offenders with offline offenders suggests few differences while online offenders often display milder symptoms. Characteristics of groomers and chat room offenders, and typologies of internet sexual offenders are also reviewed. Suggestions for future research are discussed.

Keywords: technology-involved issues, online sexual grooming, children, sexual exploitation, perpetrator

49. Knight, L., & Hester, M. (2016). Domestic violence and mental health in older adults. *International Review of Psychiatry, 28*(5), 464–474. https://doi.org/10.1080/09540261.2016.1215294

Domestic violence occurs in all age groups, but each age group might possess unique issues and experience different impacts. The present article is a review of studies on prevalence, characteristics, and the consequences of domestic violence in older adults aged 65 or older. Most findings on its prevalence suggest that the lifetime prevalence of IPV in older women is 20-30%. The rates of physical and sexual domestic abuse are lower in the older population than in the younger population while emotional abuse and controlling behaviors tend to remain stable. The influences of diminishing health and dementia in the older population might pose additional risks of victimization. Victimization from domestic violence is associated with poor physical and mental health in older adults as well. Studies on older women have indicated the increase in depression, anxiety, and other health conditions in the abused population. However, findings are conflicting about whether older victims/survivors are more influenced by domestic violence than younger victims/survivors. Alongside the negative impacts of domestic violence, older victims might also endure limited resources and opportunities as well as additional psychological burdens such as fear of loneliness. Identification and treatment of domestic violence in the older population has also been poor.

Keywords: age related factors, older adulthood, domestic violence, mental health

50. Kosson, D. S., Kelly, J. C., & White, J. W. (1997). Psychopathy-related traits predict self-reported sexual aggression among college men. *Journal of Interpersonal Violence, 12*(2), 241-254. http://dx.doi.org/10.1177/088626097012002006

Psychopathy, which has been associated with perpetration of violent offenses, consists of two distinctive dimensions: affective and interpersonal dimensions. The present study examines whether different psychopathic traits predict specific forms of sexual aggression in college male students. A total of 378 college male students were assessed on their sexually aggressive behaviors, socialization scale, and the narcissistic personality characteristics through self-report inventories; among the participants, 63 were interviewed briefly on the Psychopathy checklist. Participants were grouped into four categories based on their levels of Narcissistic personality characteristics and socialization. The results suggested that college students who displayed higher scores on psychopathy (low socialization and high narcissistic personality characteristics) reported more sexual aggression. Further analyses indicated that narcissistic characteristics and socialization predicted different forms of sexual aggression. Both socialization and Narcissistic characteristics were associated with argument, but each made unique contributions. However, only socialization was correlated with manipulative intoxication and exploitation of an intoxicated person while only narcissistic characteristics were correlated with abuse of authority. These findings support that dimensions of psychopathy predict different types of sexual aggression. Future studies might expand the links between specific psychopathic traits and specific forms of sexual aggression.

Keywords: psychopathology, psychopathy, sexual aggression, narcissistic personality, socialization

51. Krahé, B., Berger, A., Vanwesenbeeck, I., Bianchi, G., Chliaoutakis, J., Fernández-Fuertes, A. A., . . . Zygadło, A. (2015). Prevalence and correlates of young people's sexual aggression perpetration and victimisation in 10 European countries: A multi-level analysis. *Culture, Health & Sexuality, 17*(6), 682-699. http://dx.doi.org/10.1080/13691058.2014.989265

The present study examines prevalence and different levels of risk factors of perpetration and victimization of sexual aggression among young adults in Europe. Participants from 10 European countries were asked on their experience of sexually aggressive victimization and perpetration, sexual assertiveness, attitudes toward dating violence, drinking behavior, and gender equality. The analyses indicated that prevalence of at least one experience of sexual victimization ranged from 19.7% to 52.5% in young women and 10.1% to 55.8% in young men. The victimization rates were negatively associated with sexual assertiveness and positively with alcohol use in sexual interaction. Among young men, victimization rates were also correlated with lower gender equality in political power and acceptance of violence in dating relationships. Prevalence of at least one incidence of sexual perpetration ranged from 2.6% to 14.8% in young women and 5.5% to 48.7% in young men, with all countries reporting higher perpetration rates in males than in females. The perpetration rates were positively correlated with attitudes supportive of physical dating violence, alcohol use, and lower gender equalities in economic domain in men and negatively correlated with sexual assertiveness in women. Implications and limitations of the findings are discussed.

Keywords: gender factors, sexual aggression, alcohol use, sexual assertiveness, gender equality

52. Langhinrichsen-Rohling, J., & Rohling, M. (2000). Negative family-of-origin experiences: Are they associated with perpetrating unwanted pursuit behaviors? *Violence and Victims*, *15*(4), 459-471.

The present study examines the influence of family-of-origin experience on perpetration of unwanted pursuit behaviors among college students. A total of 212 college students, who recently experienced unwanted breakup with their romantic partners, were recruited. Their familiar factors (current or history of parental divorce and relationship separation, experience of interparental conflict, and witness of parental violence) and their perpetration of unwanted pursuit behaviors after breakup were assessed through self-reported, retrospective measures. The results suggested that parents' marital relationship status was correlated with the severity of unwanted pursuit behavior among male participants. Male participants with an experience of parental divorce or separation showed more severe pursuit behaviors than males without the experience and females regardless of their parents' marital relationship status. Among female participants, witness and experience of intense and threatening interparental conflict was correlated with severity of unwanted pursuit behavior. These findings suggest that negative family-of-origin experiences might influence relation behaviors during the offspring's young adulthood, with gender differences. Implications of the findings are discussed.

Keywords: pursuit behavior, relationship breakup, family of origin, parental conflict

53. Lebowitz, L., Harvey, M. R., & Herman, J. L. (1993). A stage-by-dimension model of recovery from sexual trauma. *Journal of Interpersonal Violence*, 8(3), 378-391.
http://dx.doi.org/10.1177/088626093008003006

The present article suggests a stage-by-dimension model of recovery from sexual trauma in the context of clinical treatment. Based on an ecological view of interpersonal trauma that emphasizes a complex interaction between an event, an individual, and the environment, the model integrates a three-stage model of recovery (Herman, 1992) with definitions of recovery from trauma, especially memory and self-esteem as core indicators (Harvey, 1993). The first stage of recovery aims to establish the sense of safety. Memory in this stage has several important gaps and intermittent. Self-esteem is also extremely low in this stage. The next stage focuses on integration of traumatic events and mourning over one's loss. Each client would strive to fill in the memory gaps to create a complete narrative while experience fluctuations in one's self-image. Gradually, self-loathing and self-blame would decrease. The final stage is reconnection with others. Based on the narrative, understanding of the experience is achieved. Individuals can also manage failure while avoiding self-hate. Different therapeutic approaches are necessary for different stage. Individual differences in the process of recovery and variability within recovery are referred. Implications for application of the model to treatment (screening, treatment focus, and modalities) and for future research are discussed.

Keywords: recovery, sexual violence, self-esteem, memory

54. Levenson, J. S., & Socia, K. M. (2016). Adverse childhood experiences and arrest patterns in a sample of sexual offenders. *Journal of Interpersonal Violence, 31*(10), 1883-1911. http://dx.doi.org/10.1177/0886260515570751

Experience of childhood trauma (e.g. child maltreatment or abuse; family problem) has been found to be associated with increased risk of crime offending, especially in sex offenders. The present article examines the relationship between adverse childhood experiences (ACE) and arrest patterns in sexual offenders. It was hypothesized that high ACE scores would be related to increased criminal versatility and persistence. The results showed that sex offenders commonly experienced childhood adversity in general and that high ACE scores were related to increased criminal persistence and versatility of sexual and non-sexual crimes. The effects were largest for non-sexual assault, suggesting the negative effects of childhood trauma on future violent offense perpetration. Sex offenders with adult victims also had significantly higher ACE scores and higher numbers of nonsexual arrests and total arrests than sex offenders with minor victims.

Household dysfunctions (e.g. substance abuse in the home, incarceration of a family member) predicted increased non-sexual criminal versatility and persistence while childhood sexual abuse, emotional neglect, domestic violence in childhood, and an incarcerated family member predicted increased number of sexual offenses. The findings emphasize the roles of negative childhood experience on adult criminal behaviors in sex offenders.

Keywords: family of origin, sex offense, childhood adversity, arrest

55. Levine, E. (2017). Sexual violence among middle school students: The effects of gender and dating experience. *Journal of Interpersonal Violence*, *32*(14), 2059-2082. http://dx.doi.org/10.1177/0886260515590786

Brownmiller's feminist model and the script models of sexual violence emphasize the influences from learned social gender inequalities and gendered-dynamics on individual perpetration of sexual assault. Based on these theoretical frameworks, the present article examines the effects of gender and dating experience on sexual violence among middle school students. Data were collected from 1,371 public middle school students. Analyses of the data found that participants reported similar rates of victimization by male and female peers and of perpetration against male and female peers. Also, boys were more likely to report overall victimization, victimization by female peers, overall perpetration, and perpetration against female peers; girls were more likely to report victimization by male peers and perpetration against male peers. In addition, dating experience increased the risk of girls' report of overall victimization, victimization by male peers, overall perpetration, and perpetration against male peers while increased risks of boys' report of victimization by female peers. This finding implies that many cases of adolescent sexual violence occur in different-sex relations and highlights the high occurrence of female sexual perpetration. Implications of the findings for prevention programs and future studies are discussed.

Keywords: school-based concerns, adolescent, dating, sexual violence, gender

56. McCloskey, L. A. (2013). The intergenerational transfer of mother–daughter risk for gender-based abuse. *Psychodynamic Psychiatry, 41*(2), 303-328. http://dx.doi.org/10.1521/pdps.2013.41.2.303

The present study investigates transmission of gender-based violence (experience of child sexual abuse, witness of intimate partner violence against their mothers, and experience of own intimate partner violence) across three generations and tests whether a history of violence predicts unhealthy romantic attachment styles and sexual risk taking in adolescent girls through a 10-year follow-up. The analyses of the data supported the intergenerational transmission of gendered violence. Mothers who witnessed intimate partner violence against their mothers were more likely to have experienced child sexual violence, and daughters were at higher risk of sexual abuse if their mothers experienced child sexual abuse. For the daughters, own experience of child sexual violence predicted victimization of dating violence. Daughters who had history of sexual abuse or anxious attachment style were also more likely to engage in risky sexual practices. Potential mediating factors and the mental health impacts of the cycle of abuse are presented, and the author calls for the distribution of evidence-based therapeutic interventions for girls with history of violence.

Keywords: family of origin, sexual abuse, intergenerational transmission of violence, gender-based violence, intimate partner violence

57. McQuiller Williams, L., Porter, J. L., & Smith, T. R. (2016). Understanding date rape attitudes and behaviors: Exploring the influence of race, gender, and prior sexual victimization. *Victims & Offenders*, *11*(2), 173-198. http://dx.doi.org/10.1080/15564886.2014.960025

The present study examines the effects of gender, race, and prior sexual victimization on attitudes and behaviors toward date rape in college student population. Participants' (n = 3,084) demographic variables, attitudes related to date rape, behaviors to increase the risk of date rape, and sexual victimization were collected through four waves of surveys. The results suggested that female students (compared to male students) and black students (compared to white students) experienced more negative sexual experience. Gender was a significant factor; males were more likely to display undesirable attitudes toward date rape (10 out of 13 items) and risky sexual behaviors. Females were more likely to believe that alcohol does not affect sexual their decision making. Race was also a significant factor. White participants were more likely to display undesirable attitudes (five out of 13 items) and engage in risky sexual behaviors (four out of six items) than black participants. Previous sexual victimization was positively correlated with some of the undesirable attitudes, which was unexpected. Implications and limitations of the results are discussed.

Keywords: date rape, attitude, gender, sexual victimization

58. Mercado, C. C., & Ogloff, J. R. P. (2007). Risk and the preventive detention of sex offenders in Australia and the United States. *International Journal of Law and Psychiatry, 30*(1), 49-59. http://dx.doi.org/10.1016/j.ijlp.2006.02.001

The present article reviews literature to examine whether current knowledge about sexual offenders and risk assessment tools have advanced enough to help court decisions about commitment of sexual offenders. First, indefinite period of preventive detention of a sexual offender in the U.S. and Australia, which generally accompany clinicians' evaluations of their risk of sexual reoffending, are summarized. Next, baseline sexual recidivism rates of sexual offender, predictors of reoffending, treatment efficacy, and validity of assessment instruments are reviewed. Contrary to public belief, the base-line recidivism rates of sexual offenders are usually under 40%, which is lower than those of other offender groups. Individual variables that are relevant to sexual reoffending (e.g. deviant sexual fantasies and antisocial traits) and irrelevant to reoffending (e.g. history of childhood sexual abuse and psychopathologies) are introduced. Cognitive-behavioral approaches and pharmacotherapies appear to reduce recidivism rates. Next, different types of risk assessment methods (actuarial approaches, adjusted actuarial approaches, and empirically guided or structured clinical judgments; assessment of static risks versus dynamic risks) and examples of each type are presented. The roles of psychopathy on treatment implications are also discussed. Finally, controversy over application of assessment data to detention decision, recommendations for future practice, and conclusions are illustrated.

Keywords: psychopathology, sexual offender, risk assessment, recidivism, preventive detention

59. Morgan, W., & Gilchrist, E. (2010). Risk assessment with intimate partner sex offenders. *Journal of Sexual Aggression, 16*(3), 361-372. http://dx.doi.org/10.1080/13552600.2010.502976

Intimate partner (IP) sex offenders constitute a heterogeneous population, and a lack of unification in the fields poses additional challenges to the practitioners working with offenders. The purpose of the article is to provide a summary of related research areas of interest and suggestions about risk assessment in IP sex offenders. The introduced research issues include: prevalence of IP sex abuse and its relation to child sexual abuse; the issues of detecting IPV and applying the power and control wheel as an assessment and education tool for the offenders; different typology of offenders based on generality of abuse, severity of abuse, and psychopathology;

personality dysfunctions, especially borderline personality organization, as a heighted risk of offense. Practice recommendations are described based on the literature: attainment of a holistic view of offender including types and patterns of sexual offending and selection of appropriate assessment tools by combining of sex offense assessment tools and IPV risk assessment tools.

Keywords: psychopathology, intimate partner violence, sexual offense, risk assessment

60. Nason, E. E., & Yeater, E. A. (2012). Sexual attitudes mediate the relationship between sexual victimization history and women's response effectiveness. *Journal of Interpersonal Violence*, 27(13), 2565-2581. http://dx.doi.org/10.1177/0886260512436393

Prior studies have suggested that women's abilities to respond effectively to sexually risk situations are linked to reduction in risk of unwanted experience. However, little is known about what contributes to individual differences in their response effectiveness. The present study investigates the roles of sexual attitudes on the relationship between history of sexual victimization and efficiency of women's response to dating and social situations. The participants listened to audios of low-risk or high-risk situations and were shown a video of an actor making a verbal request. Their responses were observed and recorded. Then, they completed measures about their victimization history, sexual attitudes, and psychopathology. Finally, participants were shown their own responses and rated their effectiveness at reducing the risk of unwanted sexual experience. Participants' responses were also analyzed by the experts. The results indicated that victimization history alone did not predict response effectiveness; however, experience of sexual victimization was associated with more liberal sexual attitudes, which predicted less effective strategies to decrease sexual risks in both low- and high-risk situations. Psychopathology was not associated with response effectiveness. Participants also rated their own responses to be more effective than the experts did. Implications of the findings are discussed.

Keywords: family of origin, psychopathology, sexual victimization, sexual violence, sexual attitudes

61. Ngo, Q. M., Veliz, P. T., Kusunoki, Y., Stein, S. F., & Boyd, C. J. (2018). Adolescent sexual violence: Prevalence, adolescent risks, and violence characteristics. *Preventive Medicine: An International Journal Devoted to Practice and Theory, 116*, 68-74. http://dx.doi.org/10.1016/j.ypmed.2018.08.032

Research on adolescent sexual violence has focused on dating violence, or perpetration against particular romantic partners, and their associations with familiar experience; thus, little is known about peer-to-peer sexual violence. To address this gap, the present article aims to investigate prevalence and risk factors of adolescent, peer-to-peer sexual violence in a large, diverse community sample. Participants were adolescents from public middle and high schools in Southern Michigan. Their experience of different types of sexual violence perpetration and victimization, mental health problems, substance use problems, and sociodemographics were assessed. The analyses of the data indicated that 33.9% of male adolescents and 53.5% of female adolescents reported sexual victimization; 22.8% of males and 12.6% of females reported sexual perpetration. Although the majority of reported sexual violence was perpetrated by an opposite-sex peer, same-sex violence was not uncommon. Identified risk factors for perpetration and victimization in both genders included: black racial identity, going to school in a low socioeconomic neighborhood, Substance abuse, Depression, and Attention Deficit Hyperactivity Disorder. Conduct disorder also predicted greater risk of perpetration of sexual violence among male participants. The findings contribute to understanding of statistics and risk factors of adolescent sexual violence. Implications for prevention programs are discussed.

School-based concerns, Keywords: adolescent, sexual violence, psychopathology, risk factors

62. Nichols, K. (2018). Moving beyond ideas of laddism: Conceptualising 'mischievous masculinities' as a new way of understanding everyday sexism and gender relations. *Journal of Gender Studies*, 27(1), 73-85.
http://dx.doi.org/10.1080/09589236.2016.1202815

Lad culture, most prominent in British sport places, is associated with masculinity and sexist attitudes, yet often framed as acceptable. To deepen our understanding of this culture, the present study collected ethnographic data through casual interviews at a Rugby Union club in England. The interviews were analyzed through a feminist perspective. Analyses of the interview indicated that the rugby space was considered acceptable to behave accordingly to laddism. A banter, or a sexist joke was essential to prove their lad, masculine identities and allegiance to the group. Banter was also a way to convey sexist idea and maintain male privilege in the context. Contrary to previous conceptualizations, however, laddism was not always associated with a particular type of personalities of a lad; the participants were able to actively negotiate their gender identities and act out their gender. In addition, through banter, the participants were able to display their agency, to engage in the group regardless of their age, and to challenge sexism. To move beyond limitations of current conceptualization of laddism as depicted in media and sports, an alternative way of understanding, mischievous masculinities, is suggested.

Keywords: gender factors, laddism, masculinity, sexism

63. Novack, S. (2017). Sex ed in higher ed: Should we say yes to "affirmative consent"? *Studies in Gender and Sexuality*, *18*(4), 302-312. http://dx.doi.org/10.1080/15240657.2017.1383074

The present article discusses the concept and limitations of affirmative consent as a strategy against sexual violence on college campuses through a psychoanalytic perspective. To respond to the college sex crisis, affirmative consent has been accepted nationally as the central concept of sexual assault policy. The consent policy requires a clear, positive, and voluntary communication between individuals before engagement in sexual acts. This policy attempts to transform sexuality, which is private, elusive, and often ambiguous, into an understandable, clear, recognizable psychological existence that can be communicated to others. However, this paradox makes the concept of consent inappropriate in discussion of sex. Due to its otherness, ambiguity, and multiplicity sexuality is inherently enigmatic and hidden, often to the individuals themselves. A question arises how individuals would notice their sexual desires and communicate them to their partners. The frightening, transgressing nature of sexual relationship calls for an unconscious desire for regulation; however, regulation through the consent policy might bring more confusion and risks. A vignette is presented to show challenges to elucidate sexual experience through language. Then, suggestions for developmental, educative, and existential considerations about articulating sexual desires are discussed to appropriately capture their elusive, confusing natures while setting rules and regulations.

Keywords: sexual assault, college campus, affirmative consent, sexual desire

64. Ohlert, J., Seidler, C., Rau, T., Fegert, J., & Allroggen, M. (2017). Comparison of psychopathological symptoms in adolescents who experienced sexual violence as a victim and/or as a perpetrator. *Journal of Child Sexual Abuse: Research, Treatment, & Program Innovations for Victims, Survivors, & Offenders, 26*(4), 373-387. http://dx.doi.org/10.1080/10538712.2017.1283652

Victims of sexual abuse are at high risk of developing psychopathology, and a high ratio of adolescent sexual perpetrators also report experience of sexual victimization themselves. The present study examines psychopathology in the victim-perpetrator population by comparing victim-perpetrator group with victim-only, perpetrator-only, and no-experience groups on their internalizing and externalizing symptoms. A total of 277 adolescents from national institutions were recruited and surveyed on their internalizing and externalizing symptoms and experience of sexual victimization and/or perpetration. The results suggest that adolescent with either sexual victimization or sexual perpetration exhibited higher total problem (psychopathology) scores than those without experience. Adolescents with victimization experience showed higher scores for internalizing symptoms than perpetrators and non-experience group, who did not show significant differences in internalizing scores. Adolescents with perpetration experience showed higher scores for externalizing symptoms than victims and non-experience group, who did not show significant differences in externalizing scores. Victim-perpetrator exhibited higher scores on internalizing behavior including anxiety and depression than group without experience, but lower scores than victim-only group. Explanations of the results and implications for future treatment programs are outlined.

Keywords: sexual violence, psychopathology, victim-perpetrator

65. Pashang, S., Khanlou, N., & Clarke, J. (2018). The mental health impact of cyber sexual violence on

youth identity. *International Journal of Mental Health and Addiction*. Advance online publication. http://dx.doi.org/10.1007/s11469-018-0032-4

Nowadays, youth identities are influenced by the adolescents' use of digital technologies and cyber social experience, which might sometimes inflict negative consequences in the forms of cyber sexual violence. While girls and women are at greater risk of victimization from cyber violence, their gendered nature has not been emphasized and recognized. The present study examines the effects of experience of cyber sexual violence on identity of emerging young women (EYW) through an anti-oppression approach and a gender-formative health promotion framework. Qualitative data were obtained from in-depth interviews, artwork-making, and discussion with EYWs who directly or indirectly experienced cyber sexual violence. Analyses of the data identified different themes: definition and terminology of cyber sexual violence, demographic variables of the survivors, identified cyber perpetrator, mental health impacts such as social isolation and self-blaming, and cyber revenge in the form of response to cyber sexual violence. The findings suggest that cyber sexual violence has complex, long-lasting effects on mental health of the survivors. Yet, legislative regulations are not sufficient to respond to and prevent cyber violence. Recommendations for future education, clinical practice, and policy are described.

Keywords: age related factors, cyber sexual violence, young adulthood, identity

66. Piccigallo, J. R., Lilley, T. G., & Miller, S. L. (2012). "it's cool to care about sexual violence": Men's experiences with sexual assault prevention. *Men and Masculinities*, *15*(5), 507-525. http://dx.doi.org/10.1177/1097184X12458590

The present study examines male college students' engagement in all-male anti-rape prevention programs and the potential effects of program on behavioral change. In-depth interviews with 25 active members of rape prevention groups from 11 campuses were analyzed through a ground-based approach. Analyses of the interview identified several main themes centered on engagement of the participants in the program on four different levels: (1) making sexual assault as a personal issue, (2) the importance of non-confrontational approach as men as potential allies and acknowledgement of their potential victimhood, (3) importance of the male approacher or having a man talk to another man, and (4) creation of a new social context. Example stories, limitations, effective strategies, and other relevant influences on each level are described. The findings indicate the importance of approaching in non-confrontational, alliance-building fashion by other men and the roles of peer-groups to encourage male students' engagement in rape prevention groups. As a result of their involvement in the programs, participants reported growth in knowledge of sexual violence, empathy toward rape survivors, and motivations in prevention programs. Peer-based and single-sex characteristics of the programs might also allude the programs' potential effects on behavioral changes among participant.

Keywords: male ally, rape prevention, sexual violence

67. Pina, A., Holland, J., & James, M. (2017). The malevolent side of revenge porn proclivity: Dark personality traits and sexist ideology. *International Journal of Technoethics, 8*(1), 30-43. http://dx.doi.org/10.4018/IJT.2017010103

Revenge porn is a technology-facilitated sexual violence which might cause negative psychological and social consequences in the victims. The present study examines personality characteristics of perpetrators of revenge porn and estimates behavioral proclivity of engagement in revenge porn. Participants included 100 adults recruited through advertisement on social media. Their revenge porn propensity and endorsement of Dark Triad (psychopathy, narcissism, and Machiavellianism), sadism, and ambivalent sexist beliefs were measured. Additional scales of revenge porn enjoyment and approval were also developed. The findings indicated a correlation between behavioral proclivity of revenge porn and Dark Triad and ambivalent sexism. Contrary to hypothesis, sadism was not associated with revenge porn proclivity. A majority of the participants were also found to enjoy and approve of revenge porn. Further analyses suggest that among the Dark triad, only psychopathy independently predicted revenge porn propensity. However, psychopathy was not correlated with revenge porn enjoyment or approval while

Machiavellianism predicted revenge porn approval. Narcissism was found to have significant correlations with revenge porn enjoyment. Implications of the findings and directions for future research are discussed.

Keywords: technology-involved issues, Dark Triad, sexism, sadism, revenge pornography

68. Polaschek, D. L. L., Ward, T., & Hudson, S. M. (1997). Rape and rapists: Theory and treatment. *Clinical Psychology Review, 17*(2), 117-144. http://dx.doi.org/10.1016/S0272-7358(96)00048-7

The article is a comprehensive review of literature about rape, addressing its definition, prevalence, classifications and characteristics of offenders, theoretical frameworks of etiology, and treatment issues. Studies have found that the characteristics of rapists are similar to those of general violent offenders rather than the characteristics of child molesters. Whether rapists comprise a distinctive group in the offender population is still an issue. In addition, despite the proliferation of theories that attempt to explain the etiology of rape, the field lacks an integrative theory, resulting in explanatory gaps. Nevertheless, the theories identify adverse childhood experiences and biological influences as common vulnerabilities. Treatment programs tend not to differentiate groups of sexual offenders, and a majority of programs focus on child molesters. Although it is not sure whether rapists in the treatment programs can fully meet their needs, evaluation of treatment effectiveness of sexual offenders suggests small but positive effects on rapists' recidivism rates. The authors propose that future treatment tailor to the specific needs of the rapists, such as emotional processing skills or distortions in cognitions. Development of assessment tools with higher validity to identify rapists and rigorous evaluation of the treatment programs is also suggested.

Keywords: psychopathology, sexual violence, rape, etiology, treatment

69. Pryor, D. W., & Hughes, M. R. (2013). Fear of rape among college women: A social psychological analysis. *Violence and Victims, 28*(3), 443-465. http://dx.doi.org/10.1891/0886-6708.VV-D-12-00029

The present article examines the psychological sources of fear of rape in college women in a multi-campus sample. Participants' perception of vulnerability to rape (unique invulnerability, gender risk, ability to defend self, attribution of injury, and anticipatory stigmatization) and object crime exposure (prior rape or sexual assault victimization, previous noncontact personal victimization, and structural risk of rape) were examined as potential influences on the degree of fear of rape. Distinctions were made within current and anticipatory fear of rape: by stranger or by acquaintance; at night or anytime; on campus or anywhere. The analyses of the data suggested that fear of rape combines each individual's subjective and objective risks. Perception of unique invulnerability and ability to defend self were negatively correlated with fear of rape while perception of gender risk, trauma, and stigma of rape were positively correlated. Limited effects of past sexual victimization and current structural risk. The participants were more fearful of rape by strangers than by known offenders. In fact, fear of stranger rape was perceived to be higher than the actual risk while fear of acquaintance rape was perceived to be lower. Future research directions based on the findings are described.

Keywords: fear of rape, college population, sexual violence

70. Ramsey-Klawsnik, H. (2003). Elder sexual abuse within the family. *Journal of Elder Abuse & Neglect, 15*(1), 43-58.
http://dx.doi.org/10.1300/J084v15n01_04

In the present study, one hundred cases of elder sexual abuse between 1993 and 2002, which involve family members of the victims/survivors as perpetrators, were investigated and analyzed qualitatively through clinical consultation records. The cases were categorized into two groups based on the relationship between the perpetrators and the victims/survivors: marital sexual abuse and incestuous abuse. Three types of marital sexual abuse were identified for both female and male victims/survivors: long-lasting domestic sexual abuse, which is the most frequently observed; recent onset of sexual abuse in a long-term marital relationship, which was infrequently observed; sexual abuse in a new romantic relationship, the least commonly observed. The categorization of incestuous abuse cases depended on the perpetrator types: adult offspring (usually sons abusing their mothers), relatives, and quasi-relatives. In some cases, offenders were juvenile. Further analyses of clinical dynamics of the cases indicated the range of abusive behaviors, causes and risk factors of the abuse, and forensic markers or signs of the elderly sexual abuse. Implications of the findings are discussed.

Keywords: age related factors, elder sexual abuse, domestic abuse, incestuous abuse

71. Rebocho, M. F., & Gonçalves, R. A. (2012). Sexual predators and prey: A comparative study of the hunting behavior of rapists and child molesters. *Journal of Interpersonal Violence*, 27(14), 2770-2789. http://dx.doi.org/10.1177/0886260512438280

Hunting behavior in criminals is a complex decision-making process, as offenders take various factors into account. The present article compares rapist and child molester on their hunting behavior patterns and modus operandi characteristics. Incarcerated sex offenders who displayed hunting behavior were interviewed, and their hunting style, victim selection, attack method, approach strategies, and geographic variables were analyzed. Three clusters in offenders were identified: manipulative, opportunist, and coercive. The manipulative type, mostly child molesters, was characterized by premediated crimes which targeted known victims. The offenders were less likely to inflict harm on the victims, and their offenses were also likely to occur in indoor areas. The opportunist type, including both child molesters and rapists, was characterized by non-premediated crimes which targeted both strangers and known victims. The offenders tended to use vehicle for offense, and their offenses occurred in multiple, remote locations. The coercive type, mostly rapists, was characterized by non-premediated crimes which targeted strangers and employment of coercion. The offenders often used weapons and tended to inflict severe harm on the victims. These findings contribute to deeper understanding of offense characteristics in different types of sexual offenders and might guide development of effective strategies for sexual violence prevention and intervention programs.

Keywords: typology of sexual offenders, sexual violence, offender, offense characteristics

72. Rice, M. E., & Harris, G. T. (2014). What does it mean when age is related to recidivism among sex offenders? *Law and Human Behavior, 38*(2), 151-161. http://dx.doi.org/10.1037/lhb0000052

Although the older age of a sexual offender has been found correlated with better outcomes and lower recidivism rates, how age affects recidivism rates and risk factors has not been fully investigated yet. The present article examines the relationship between age of and recidivism in sexual offenders in two studies. In the first study, age at index offense, age at release, and other risk factors of sexual offenders aged over 50 at release and their sexual and violent recidivism were measured. Age at index offense was correlated with sexual and violent recidivism while age at release reached marginal significance. In the second study, sexual offenders' violent recidivism, their age at first offense, age at index offense, age at release, PCL-R (Hare, 2003) scores, and SORAG (Quinsey, et al., 2006) scores were measured. Age at first offense had the strongest validity contribution to the recidivism rates above other established predictors while age at release had the least. These results suggest that age at release might be a poor predictor of sexual or violent recidivism, especially compared to age of first offense.

Keywords: sexual offender, recidivism, age related factors,

73. Richardson, E. W., Simons, L. G., & Futris, T. G. (2017). Linking family-of-origin experiences and perpetration of sexual coercion: College males' sense of entitlement. *Journal of Child and Family Studies, 26*(3), 781-791. http://dx.doi.org/10.1007/s10826-016-0592-5

Sexual coercion is a prevalent practice in college campus, and family-of-origin factors have been investigated as the core risk factors of its perpetration. The present article examines the relationship between family-of-origin factors (interparental relationship quality and parenting practices) and perpetration of sexual coercion in college male population, with potential mediating effects by the sense of entitlement. Self-report data from 326 male college students were collected on interparental warmth, interparental hostility, overparenting, inconsistent parenting, entitlement, and sexual coercion. Data analyses suggested that hostility between parents was significantly related to sense of entitlement and perpetration of sexual coercion in sons. Negative parenting practices were also indirectly related to perpetration of sexual coercion through the sense of entitlement. Although interparental warmth was not related to perpetration of sexual coercion, it was positively associated with overparenting. The findings suggest that educational programs for parents might need to address the effects of parental relationship qualities and positive parenting practices on the offspring, which might help to reduce the intergenerational transmission of violence.

Keywords: sexual coercion, family of origin, entitlement, young adulthood

74. Roberts, A. L., Koenen, K. C., Lyall, K., Robinson, E. B., & Weisskopf, M. G. (2015). Association of autistic traits in adulthood with childhood abuse, interpersonal victimization, and posttraumatic stress. *Child Abuse & Neglect, 45*, 135-142. http://dx.doi.org/10.1016/j.chiabu.2015.04.010

Children with autistic traits has been found to be at higher risk of victimization from abuse and more likely to experience PTSD following a traumatic event. The present study investigates prevalence of childhood abuse or other trauma victimization and PTSD symptoms among adult women with varying degrees of autistic traits. Participants' experience of traumatic events including childhood abuse, autistic traits, and PTSD symptoms were assessed. Based on their severity of autistic traits, participants were grouped into quintiles for between-group comparison. The results suggested that women with highest autistic traits were more likely to experience childhood sexual abuse, childhood physical or emotional abuse, mugging, pressure into sexual contact, and more severe PTSD symptoms compared to women with lowest autistic traits. However, they were not more likely to experience sexual harassment at work. The more frequent childhood exposure to abuse in participants with high autistic traits accounted for about one-third of the increased PTSD symptoms associated with autistic traits. Implications of the findings are discussed.

Keywords: emerging issues: vulnerable populations, childhood abuse, sexual harassment, PTSD, autistic traits

75. Rodgers, K. B., & Hust, S. J. T. (2018). Sexual objectification in music videos and acceptance of potentially offensive sexual behaviors. *Psychology of Popular Media Culture*, 7(4), 413-428. http://dx.doi.org/10.1037/ppm0000142

Music videos often feature sexual images of women to present either female sexual objectification or empowerment. The present study examines how female adolescents and young adults understand music media that depict female sexuality and whether their understanding of the media is correlated with their acceptance of potentially offensive sexual behaviors (POSB) by male peers. A total of 259 female teenagers and young adults were shown a randomly selected music video. Their perceptions of contents in the music video, attitudes toward female sexual objectification, and perception of POSB were recorded. Analyses of the data indicated college women were more likely to perceive the women in the music video to be attractive and powerful. Also, participants rated the women in the music video to be more attractive when they were perceived to be sexual objects but not when they were perceived to be powerful. Contrary to hypotheses, participants' perception of music video was not significantly correlated with their experience of POSB. However, among participants who were more accepting of sexual objectification, being more entertained by the music videos or perceiving the music video to be more realistic was negatively associated with being offended by POSB. Implications of the findings are discussed.

Keywords: technology-involved issues, sexual objectification, media, potentially offensive sexual behavior, adolescents and young adulthood

76. Romero-Sánchez, M., Carretero-Dios, H., Megías, J. L., Moya, M., & Ford, T. E. (2017). Sexist humor and rape proclivity: The moderating role of joke teller gender and severity of sexual assault. *Violence Against Women*, *23*(8), 951-972. http://dx.doi.org/10.1177/1077801216654017

Prejudiced norm theory posits that sexist humor allows men to express their sexist attitudes, including rape proclivity, against women. To further investigate this effect, the present study examines the effects of sexist humor on male's self-reported rape proclivity (RP) in three experiments using rape scenarios. In Experiment 1, hypotheses on gender of the joke teller and degree of physical violence depicted in the scenario on the effects of sexist joke were tested in hypothetical rape scenarios. As hypothesized, men with higher in hostile sexism reported greater RP upon exposure to sexist jokes only when a woman (versus a man) delivered the jokes. Also, this relationship between hostile sexism and gender of the joke teller was significant only in moderate violence scenarios. In high violence scenarios, only participants' hostile sexism was positively related to self-reported RP. In Experiment 2, whether the effects of sexist jokes on RP on scenarios can be generalized to women in general was tested. As hypothesized, upon exposure to sexist jokes told by women, participants with high hostile sexism reported RP generalized to broader women. These findings might imply that sexist humor can foster an environment that accepts rape culture.

Keywords: sexist joke, rape proclivity, gender, hostile sexism

77. Scarpati, A. S., & Pina, A. (2017). Cultural and moral dimensions of sexual aggression: The role of moral disengagement in men's likelihood to sexually aggress. *Aggression and Violent Behavior, 37,* 115-121. http://dx.doi.org/10.1016/j.avb.2017.09.001

The present article examines the roles of moral values and social norms on individuals' engagement in and justification of sexual aggression through a narrative review of past studies. Theories on moral are reviewed on universality and relativity of morality, different ethics, definition of morality, and moral judgment. Social norms inform the people what behaviors are acceptable (or inacceptable) and guide people's thoughts and behavior. Through social norms and moral standards, people learn to regulate themselves and behave humanely. However, social norms might legitimate harmful behaviors in certain situations. In a traditional, gender unequal society, some forms of gendered violence are justified as commitment to social norms and morals. In addition, despite the existence of morality, individuals might still commit detrimental behaviors through disengagement from moral regulation. According to Bandura's conceptualization of moral disengagement, individuals detach from moral standards and self-regulation through psychosocial mechanisms and justify their violent behaviors. To make the behavior appear less aggressive, offenders employ different strategies. In conclusion, social influences are crucial for individual's construction of identities and subsequent behaviors. Implications of this perspective and recommendations for future research are delineated.

Keywords: gender factors, sexual aggression, social norm, morality

78. Schwark, S. (2017). Visual representations of sexual violence in online news outlets. *Frontiers in Psychology, 8*, Article ID 774.

The present study examines visual messages conveyed through photographs in online news articles about sexual violence. Photographs published between January 2013 and March 2015 were investigated through qualitative thematic analyses. Two themes, rape myth and portrayal of victimhood, and their subthemes were identified. The rape-myth theme consisted of three sub-themes. The women in the photographs were portrayed according to Western beauty standard of females (beauty standards); there was direct presentation or implication of physical violence (physical violence); the photographs depicted outdoor scenes (location). The portrayal of victimhood consisted of five sub-themes. The victims were all shown in cringing positions and covering their faces, isolated from other people (passivity); the most photographs employed non-descriptive backgrounds without contexts (background); the perpetrators were presented in the foreground while victim/survivors in the background (organization of space); women were facing the camera while perpetrators' were turned back (camera perspective); only some body parts of the perpetrators were shown in the light, contributing the impression of "lurking in the dark" (lighting). Media not only reflect public opinion about sexual violence but also strengthen rape myths, and photographs create affective reactions in readers to encourage exposure to a news article. Recommendations for future press images are discussed.

Keywords: technology-involved issues, media, visual representation, rape myth, sexual violence

79. Seto, M. C., & Lalumière, M. L. (2010). What is so special about male adolescent sexual offending? A review and test of explanations through meta-analysis. *Psychological Bulletin, 136*(4), 526-575. http://dx.doi.org/10.1037/a0019700

Considering both general and special delinquency explanations about adolescent sexual offending, the present article aims to compare adolescent male sex offenders and adolescent male non-sex offenders on their risk factors (e.g. general delinquency risk factors, sexuality, interpersonal problems) through a meta-analysis of 59 studies from 1975 to 2008. The analyses suggested that general delinquency explanations did not fully explain sexual offending in adolescents, despite many similarities between adolescent sex offenders and non-sex offenders. Adolescent sex-offenders had less extensive criminal history and fewer substance use problems than their non-sex offender counterparts. Adolescent sex-offenders experienced more frequent sexual and physical abuse and emotional neglect or abuse. Sex offending was also associated with more social isolation, atypical sexual interests, early exposures to sexual contents, anxiety, and lower self-esteem. Among the factors, atypical sexual interests yielded the largest group differences, followed by history of sexual abuse. No difference in antisocial beliefs and attitudes about women and sexual offending, family problems, cognitive abilities, other psychopathologies and interpersonal problems was found. Implications of the findings for future research and offender assessments, treatment, and prevention approaches are described.

Keywords: school-based concerns, adolescent, sex offending, delinquency, risk factor

80. Silva, T., Woodhams, J., & Harkins, L. (2017). "An adventure that went wrong": Reasons given by convicted perpetrators of multiple perpetrator sexual offending for their involvement in the offense. *Archives of Sexual Behavior.* Advance online publication. http://dx.doi.org/10.1007/s10508-017-1011-8

Although not many studies on multiple perpetrator sexual offending (MPSO) have investigated reasons for the assault, past interviews with sexual offenders suggested non-sexual explanations such as group dynamics as critical reasons for MPSO. The present article interviews 25 perpetrators involved in MPSO for their reasons and explanations for the involvement. Thematic analysis of the interviews identified six themes as reasons for involvement in the offense: (1) started as something else, (2) influence of others (direct or indirect), (3) lack of insight about the assault, (4) victim blaming, (5) influence of alcohol and or drugs, and (6) normalized sexual violence. Participants commonly reported combinations of different themes and rarely referred to individual factors. These findings support the Multi Factorial Model of MPSO, which proposes that various levels of influences—individual, sociocultural, situational factors—and interactions among them contribute to perpetration of MPSO and emphasizes the roles of group processes (interaction between personal and situational) on the offense. Implications of the findings for future prevention, assessment, and intervention programs are described.

Keywords: typology of sexual offenders, sexual violence, multiple perpetrator sexual offending, offender

81. Simons, L. G., Burt, C. H., & Simons, R. L. (2008). A test of explanations for the effect of harsh parenting on the perpetration of dating violence and sexual coercion among college males. *Violence and Victims*, 23(1), 66-82. http://dx.doi.org/10.1891/0886-6708.23.1.66

Based on social learning theory, attachment theory, and criminological perspectives, the present article examines the relationship between family-of-origin experiences and perpetration of sexual and dating violence in adulthood with antisocial tendencies, permissive sexual attitudes, and a belief that violence is acceptable in romantic relationship as potential mediators. Male participants were surveyed on harsh corporal punishment, trust/support in parent-child relationships, dating violence, sexual coercion, antisocial traits, sexually permissive attitudes, and belief that violence is a legitimate component of romantic relationship. Analyses of the data suggest that negative parenting increases the risk of sexual coercion and dating violence indirectly through promoting antisocial tendencies, sexually permissive attitudes, and the notion of violence as a legitimate part of romantic relationship. Both harsh corporal punishment and low parent-child relationship quality predicted development of the belief that violence is legitimate in romantic relationship, which was associated with perpetration of both sexual coercion and dating violence. Harsh corporal punishment also had a direct effect on perpetration of dating violence. Low parental trust and support predicted sexually permissive attitudes, which were associated with perpetration of sexual coercion. A general antisocial orientation predicted perpetration of only sexual coercion. The results are discussed in comparison to findings of past studies.

Keywords: family of origin, sexual coercion, dating violence, abusive parenting, antisocial tendency

82. Simons, L. G., Simons, R. L., Lei, M.-K., & Sutton, T. E. (2012). Exposure to harsh parenting and pornography as explanations for males' sexual coercion and females' sexual victimization. *Violence*

*and Victims, 27*(3), 378-395.
http://dx.doi.org/10.1891/0886-6708.27.3.378

Past studies have supported the associations of family-of-origin factors and consumption of sexually explicit images with sexual coercion. The present study examines how exposure to corporal punishment, paternal aggression and rejection, and consumption of pornographic images might be associated with increased perpetration of sexual coercion in males and with acceptance of unwanted sexual practices in females. The results suggest that experience of frequent corporal punishment was associated with increased perpetration of sexual coercion in men only with high consumption of pornographic images. For women with high consumption of pornographic images, the experience of sexual victimization was high regardless of family-of-origin factors. For women with low consumption of pornographic images, however, father's hostility was positively associated with experience of sexual coercion. Experience of frequent corporal punishment was also associated with increased experience of sexual victimization in women. Implications of the findings for policies, prevention programs, and future studies to reduce sexual violence are described.

Keywords: family of origin, sexual coercion, corporal punishment, paternal aggression, pornography

83. Soylu, N., Ayaz, M., Gökten, E. S., Alpaslan, A. H., Dönmez, Y. E., Özcan, Ö. Ö., . . . Tufan, A. E. (2016). Gender differences in sexually abused children and adolescents: A multicenter study in Turkey. *Journal of*

*Child Sexual Abuse: Research, Treatment, & Program Innovations for Victims, Survivors, & Offenders*, 25(4), 415-427.
http://dx.doi.org/10.1080/10538712.2016.1143073

The present article investigates gender differences in abuse-related characteristics and post-abuse disorders among child and adolescent victims/survivors of sexual violence. Data were collected from 1,250 minor sexual violence victim/survivors on their sociodemographic variables, mental disorder diagnoses, characteristics of the offense, and intelligence levels. The analyses suggest that about 80% of the victims were girls and the other 20% were boys. The most prevalent form of sexual violence among girls was sexual touch, while it was anal penetration among boys. Sexual violence against boys was also more likely to accompany force and physical violence. Abusers of sexual violence against girls were more likely to be a family member, a familiar person, or multiple perpetrators. For both girls and boys, most of the abusers were male. 70% of girls and 56% of boys reported at least one mental disorder after victimization from the sexual abuse. Boys and girls experienced similar rates of post-abuse acute stress disorder, PTSD, and conduct disorder. Girls were more likely to experience depression while boys were more likely to have intellectual disability. These findings are discussed in comparison of past findings.

Keywords: child sexual violence, mental disorder, gender factors

84. Starfelt, L. C., Young, R. M., White, K. M., & Palk, G. R. M. (2015). Explicating the role of sexual coercion and vulnerability alcohol expectancies in rape attributions. *Journal of Interpersonal Violence*, *30*(11), 1965-1981. http://dx.doi.org/10.1177/0886260514549466

The present study investigates the effects of alcohol expectancies (sexual coercion and sexual vulnerabilities scales, and self-oriented versus other-oriented) on people's rape blame attribution. It was hypothesized that stronger expectancies would be related to lesser perpetrator blame and greater victim blame. A total of 175 young adults were measured on their demographics, including alcohol consumption, traditional gender role attitudes, and rape myth acceptance. They read a scenario that involved intoxication and rape, and their responses to the scenario (blameworthiness of the perpetrator and victim) and alcohol expectancies were assessed. The analyses of the data indicated that participants regarded the situation as a rape. Consistent with hypotheses, stronger alcohol expectancies were associated with lower perpetrator blame and greater victim blame. Specifically, self-oriented expectancies, sexual coercion expectancy, and rape myth acceptance explained a significant variance of perpetrator blame while other-oriented expectancies, sexual coercion expectancy, and rape myth acceptance explained victim blame. These effects remained significant after controlling for gender role attitudes and rape myth acceptance. This finding might imply that different cognitive processes underlie judgment of perpetrators and victims.

Keywords: rape, alcohol expectancy, vulnerability, sexual coercion

85. Süssenbach, P., Eyssel, F., Rees, J., & Bohner, G. (2017). Looking for blame: Rape myth acceptance and attention to victim and perpetrator. *Journal of Interpersonal Violence*, 32(15), 2323-2344. http://dx.doi.org/10.1177/0886260515591975

The present article investigates the effects of rape myth acceptance (RMA) on individuals' biased information search about victims and perpetrators in alleged rape case scenarios in two experiments. In Study 1, participants were provided with an alleged male-to-female rape case vignette and asked to select additional information either about the potential defendant or potential victim. Participants' RMA was associated with preference to information relevant to victims. In Study 2, participants were presented with a rape case and shown a photograph of both victim and perpetrator. Their eye movements were recorded while they were gazing at the photograph. Participants' RMA was associated with the time they spent on observing the victim rather than the perpetrator. In both studies, higher RMA was associated with pro-defendant and anti-victim judgments, which were consistent with previous findings. The findings of present article support that RMA guides individuals' attention away from perpetrators to the victims in rape cases. Implications and suggestions for future research are discussed.

Keywords: gender factors, rape myth acceptance, information search, eye movement, rape

86. Sutton, T. E., & Simons, L. G. (2015). Sexual assault among college students: Family of origin hostility, attachment, and the hook-up culture as risk factors. *Journal of Child and Family Studies*, *24*(10), 2827-2840. http://dx.doi.org/10.1007/s10826-014-0087-1

The present article examines insecure attachment styles, negative family-of-origin experiences, and engagement in hook-up culture as risk factors for sexual assault perpetration in men and victimization in women. 624 college students were surveyed on interparental hostility, harsh parenting, attachment style, sociosexuality, alcohol use, and hook-up frequency, men's sexual assault perpetration, and women's sexual assault victimization. Analyses of the data suggested that interparental hostility was significantly related to an avoidant attachment style while harsh parenting was related to an anxious attachment style. Family-of-origin factors were indirectly related to sexual assault perpetration or victimization through insecure attachment styles and participation in the hook-up culture. For men, experience of harsh parenting was indirectly related with perpetration of sexual assault through to greater participation in hook-up culture. For women, experience of harsh parenting was indirectly related to sexual assault victimization through anxious attachment style. An avoidant attachment style was positively to engagement in hook-up culture while anxious attachment was not related. Participation in hook-up culture was positively related to sexual assault perpetration in men and victimization in women. Implications of the results for educational programs for establishment of healthy relationship among parents and young adults are described.

Keywords: family of origin, sexual assault, attachment style, hook-up culture, young adulthood

87. Totten, M. (2003). Girlfriend abuse as a form of masculinity construction among violent, marginal male youth. *Men and Masculinities*, 6(1), 70-92. http://dx.doi.org/10.1177/1097184X03253138

The present article investigates development of masculine identities among marginalized, abusive male adolescents and the effects of familiar and gender ideologies. Participants were 30 abusive individuals who all came from marginalized background and reported individual or collective behaviors against a girlfriend, racial or sexual minorities. The participants' images of an ideal man, consistent with the rigid definition of masculinity, were inseparable from their belief of an ideal, traditional family. Despite their lost access to traditional benefits associated with patriarchy, a significant number of the participants supported traditional, patriarchal-authoritarian belief and violence against women. To compensate for this situation, the participants defended and proved their masculinities through overt domination over women and homosexual males. Participants often justified their reported violent behaviors to be non-abusive or to be grounded on the superior moral plane. Participants were also likely to have witnessed father's violence against mother and experienced abuse from fathers. Nevertheless, participants differed on their embracement of patriarchal-authoritarian perspective. These differences explained the variation in the degree of violence against girlfriends or other minorities. The findings support the roles of familial and gender ideologies on construction of masculinity. Implications for social policy, research, and intervention programs are discussed.

Keywords: identity formation, masculinity, gendered violence, patriarchy, heterosexism

88. Turchik, J. A., Hebenstreit, C. L., & Judson, S. S. (2016). An examination of the gender inclusiveness of current theories of sexual violence in adulthood: Recognizing male victims, female perpetrators, and same-sex violence. *Trauma, Violence, & Abuse, 17*(2), 133-148.
http://dx.doi.org/10.1177/1524838014566721

Recognizing that both men and women can be victims and offenders of sexual violence, the present article aims to investigate the need for a gender-inclusive model of sexual aggression that considers risk factors of victimization and perpetration in both genders, review current theories regarding their gender-inclusivity, and recommend future directions to increase gender-inclusiveness. Most of the current models and theories of sexual assault and social prevention, treatment, and advocacy programs are based on male perpetrators, female victims, and their heterosexuality. This has caused less awareness and resources for male victims and victims in non-heterosexual relationship, limiting their chance to receive treatment and relevant services. Next, biological, psychological, social, and integrated theories are reviewed on their empirical evidence, gender inclusiveness, and applications in studies. The theories differ in compatibility with gender inclusive conceptualization of sexual violence. For example, routine activity theory does not assume the gender of the offender or a victim, and the theory has been used to examine female perpetrators, male victims. Also, integrating different theories might increase explanatory power and increase our understanding of sexual violence. Future directions to adopt gender inclusive conceptualization in research, clinical practice, and advocacy are suggested.

Keywords: gender factors, gender inclusive, male victims, female perpetrator, sexual violence

89. Van Bruggen, L. K., Runtz, M. G., & Kadlec, H. (2006). Sexual Revictimization: The role of sexual self-esteem and dysfunctional sexual behaviors. *Child Maltreatment, 11*(2), 131-145. http://dx.doi.org/10.1177/1077559505285780

Individuals who experience victimization from an early sexual assault are at greater vulnerabilities of later sexual revictimization. Studies have suggested the influence of child sexual abuse (CSA) on survivors' sexual attitudes and behaviors during adolescence and adulthood might increase the chance for revictimization. The present article examines the relationship between child maltreatment including CSA and later experience of sexual assault and the roles of sexual attitudes and behaviors on the relationship. A total of 402 female college students were assessed on their maltreatment history, sexual self-esteem, sexual concerns, risky sexual behaviors, and experience of sexual assault after age of 14. The results indicated that participants with experience of CSA and child psychological maltreatment (CPM) had lower self-esteem and greater sexual concerns. Participants with CSA history were also twice more likely to experience later sexual assault than those without CSA. However, contrary to hypotheses, participants with CSA were not more likely to display uncommitted/dysfunctional sexual behaviors. Further analyses through structural equation modeling revealed that sexual self-esteem, sexual concerns, and risky sexual behaviors mediated the relationship between experience of child maltreatment (CSA and CPM) and later sexual revictimization. Implications of the findings on child maltreatment and sexual health in women are discussed.

Keywords: family of origin, child sexual abuse, child psychological maltreatment, sexual attitudes, sexual behaviors

90. Van Ness, S. R. (1984). Rape as instrumental violence: A study of youth offenders. *Journal of Offender Counseling, Services & Rehabilitation, 9*(1-2), 161-170. http://dx.doi.org/10.1300/J264v09n01_11

To understand the nature of rape, present study investigates young sexual offenders and compares them with other delinquent offenders in a sample recruited from three youth correctional institutions through questionnaires and background information files. Most rapist participants reported anger events (90%) or substance abuse (55%) before their rape offense. The victims were not those whom the offenders fought with. Suggestions of premediated planning of rape were reported by 86% of the participants. Most of the victims were young women and teenage girls but male rape, targeting mostly young boys, also occurred at 32% although no rapist reported himself to be homosexual. Use of weapon was also common. Examinations of rapists' history indicated their previous use of physical violence and poor anger control skill. These implied that they were unable to exert conventional skills to cope with anger in conflicts with others, followed by continuous social role failures (as students, employees, and citizens) and removals. Moreover, rapists display poorer skills than non-rapist, violent offenders. The rapists' exposure to intra-family violence and serious neglect was suggested as a potential contributor to the difference. These findings on rapists suggest that rape might be an instrumental violence, motivated by achieving a reward.

Keywords: rapist, anger, violent offender, social skills

91. Veneziano, C., & Veneziano, L. (2002). Adolescent sex offenders: A review of the literature. *Trauma, Violence, & Abuse, 3*(4), 247-260. https://doi.org/10.1177/1524838002237329

Adolescent sex offenders comprise a considerable portion in child sexual violence, and adult sexual perpetrators often report their first sexual offense to have occurred in their adolescence. Thus, the need for identification and treatment of juvenile sexual offenders is high. The present article summarizes past studies on characteristics, assessment, and treatment of adolescent sexual offenders. Juvenile sexual offenders are often victims of childhood sexual violence themselves. Other identified characteristics of juvenile sexual offenders include: a history of negative family-of-origin experience, experience of abuse, social inadequacy, difficulties at school, poor cognitive functions, and mental disorders, which are similar to characteristics of general juvenile delinquent offenders. As juvenile sexual offenders constitute a heterogeneous group, it is recommended to assess different aspects of each offender to design treatment programs tailored to individual needs of the offenders. Many treatment programs are modeled after successful programs for adult perpetrators, but more recent programs are specialized for adolescent populations. Successful treatment approaches include cognitive-behavioral techniques or more holistic approaches such as the multisystemic therapy. Evaluations of the effectiveness of treatments are still in progress, but individualized programs seem to be more effective than generic programs. Implications for future research, assessment, and treatment programs are discussed.

Keywords: school-based concerns, sexual offense, adolescent offender, treatment, assessment

92. Vonderhaar, R. L., & Carmody, D. C. (2015). There are no "innocent victims": The influence of just world beliefs and prior victimization on rape myth acceptance. *Journal of Interpersonal Violence, 30*(10), 1615-1632. http://dx.doi.org/10.1177/0886260514549196

Rape myths justify male's sexual assault and place the blame on the victims/survivors. Based on past findings of just world beliefs, prior victimization, and demographics, the present study investigates these variables as potential predictors of individuals' degree of rape myth acceptance. Data were collected from 979 university students through online survey on their previous experience of rape, gender, ethnicity, age, just world beliefs, and rape myth acceptance. Analyses of the data found that rape myth acceptance was significantly higher with higher just world beliefs, younger age, absence of rape victimization experience, male gender, and lower level of education. Rape myth acceptance was also highest among Asian/Pacific Islanders identity and lowest among White. These findings are consistent with previous findings. As rape myth is likely to impede with recovery of victims/survivors through victim-blaming, individuals with risk factors might need to be educated on consequences of rape on victims/survivors. Implications for future rape prevention programs and the legal systems are discussed.

Keywords: gender factors, rape myth acceptance, just world beliefs, demographic variables, rape victimization

93. Weare, S. (2018). From coercion to physical force: Aggressive strategies used by women against men in "forced-to-penetrate" cases in the uk. *Archives of Sexual Behavior. 47*(8), 2191-2205. http://dx.doi.org/10.1007/s10508-018-1232-5

Compared to male-to-female sexual aggression, female-to-male sexual aggression, especially forced-to-penetrate (FTP) cases—one of the more serious form of aggression—has been much less examined. To address this gap, the present article investigates women's aggressive strategies used in FTP cases through narratives of male victim/survivors. Quantitative and qualitative data were collected through a mixed-methods design through survey options regarding experience of aggressive strategies and open-ended questions. The results support existence of women's aggressive strategies toward men. Verbally coercive strategies, including blackmails, threats, coercion, and continuous verbal pressure, was the most common (33%) strategies reported by the participants. The threats also included a gendered strategy, such as threats of false rape allegation. Use of alcohol or drug to intoxicate the victims was the second common (26.8%) strategy. Physical force or use of violence was third common (19.6%) reported strategies, which contradicts previous findings. Other strategies encompass indirect coercion through power imbalance among family members or family friends and exploitation of mother's role (e.g. threat to refuse father's access to children or to terminate pregnancy). Participants also reported offenders' use of multiple strategies within one incidence. Implications of the findings and suggestions for future research are discussed.

Keywords: gender factors, sexual violence, forced-to-penetrate, male victim, female perpetrator

94. Weiler, J. V. (2015). Living in the era of digital exhibitionism. *Child & Youth Services, 36*(4), 329-344. http://dx.doi.org/10.1080/0145935X.2015.1096596

The present article summarizes different types of child and adolescent sexual abuse on the internet and presents recommendations for future practice. Four studies on abusive images of victims/survivors of online or offline abuse either by an adult or a victim and self-generated images shared beyond control are reviewed. In the online context, sexual offenders can easily access to children and adolescents while not exposing their identities; offenders might also utilize online and digital methods to connect to victims and generate sexual images of minors through different tactics. Not only adult perpetrators but also peers can record and distribute sexual images of others using cell phones. As the images are shared in the peer group, the distribution has direct and permanent impact on the victims/survivors' everyday life. The victims/survivors often feel strong sense of guilt, shame, and self-loathing for disclosing their victimization. Trusting relationship between the victims/survivors and therapists, support for the victims/survivors, and appropriate trainings for clinicians might be necessary to encourage disclosure. Children and adolescents' risk taking and protection behaviors in online contexts need to be understood to develop effective prevention programs. Recommendations for improvements of services/practice and for future studies are also described.

Keywords: technology-involved issues, online space, sexual harassment, adolescent, children

95. Worling, J. R., & Langton, C. M. (2012). Assessment and treatment of adolescents who sexually offend: Clinical issues and implications for secure settings. *Criminal Justice and Behavior, 39*(6), 814-841. http://dx.doi.org/10.1177/0093854812439378

Adolescents who sexually offend are more likely to be placed in residential correctional facilities than adolescents who non-sexually offend. Yet, studies have examined concerns associated with their institutional placement, such as less involvement of family, victimization by another youth, or difficulties meeting needs. The present article outlines recommendations for assessment and treatment to provide comprehensive clinical services for adolescent sexual offenders in the residential settings. Adolescent sex offenders constitute a heterogeneous population, and each offender has unique needs. To capture and address the needs, assessment should examine diverse areas, and individual factors identified during the assessment procedures should be reflected in treatment. Principles and tools for risk-needs assessment are described. Despite limited empirical data, results have been positive for specialized treatment programs in reducing recidivism rates in the population. Next, treatment recommendations to prevent future sexual re-offense are presented. Cognitive-behavioral approaches have been found effective to reduce shame and facilitate treatment. Issues of treatment delivery (e.g. group-based therapies in a correctional setting, manuals and books) and additional treatment goals and considerations (e.g. offenders' responsibility and accountability of offense, enhancement of healthy sexual interests and attitudes, awareness of victim impact, childhood trauma) are delineated.

Keywords: psychopathology, sexual offense, adolescent, treatment, assessment

96. Worling, J. R., & Langton, C. M. (2015). A prospective investigation of factors that predict desistance from recidivism for adolescents who have sexually offended. *Sexual Abuse: Journal of Research and Treatment*, 27(1), 127-142. http://dx.doi.org/10.1177/1079063214549260

Studies of violent offending have focused on risk factors rather than protective factors that predict desistance from violence. The present article investigates whether the validity of recidivism assessment among male adolescent sex offense can be improved by including protective factors and whether sex reoffending and non-sex reoffending have different protective factors. 81 adolescents who perpetrated sex offenses were recruited. Their risk of sexual offending was assessed on ERASOR (Worling, 2004). Their strengths were assessed on BERS (Epstein, 2004) which assesses strengths of youth in five domains: interpersonal strength, involvement with family, intrapersonal strength, school functioning, and affective strength. The recidivism rates were also gathered for the follow-up period. The analyses suggest that the recidivism rates were low for both sex offense and non-sex offense. The ERASOR was found to effectively predict the sexual recidivism. Only the Affective Strength in BERS predicted the sexual recidivism, but the effects of strength did not offer additional validity to the predictability of ERASOR scales. The BERS School Functioning score was found to effectively predict desistance from non-sex offending. These findings might imply different protective factors for sex and non-sex recidivism and the role of attachment in development of sexual offense.

Keywords: psychopathology, protective factors, adolescent, sex offending, recidivism

97. Yates, P. M., & Kingston, D. A. (2006). The self-regulation model of sexual offending: The relationship between offence pathways and static and dynamic sexual offence risk. *Sexual Abuse: Journal of Research and Treatment, 18*(3), 259-270. http://dx.doi.org/10.1177/107906320601800304

The self-regulation model suggested by Ward and Hudson (1998) is a nine-stage process of offending, developed specifically for sexual offenders. The model includes individuals' internal and external processes that contribute to behaviors relevant to inhibitory or acquisitional goals. Based on the model, four potential pathways that lead to sexual offending were suggested, addressing both between-individuals and within-individuals variables. The present study tests validity of this model within a sample of 80 adult male sexual offenders, consisted of child molesters, rapists, incest offenders, and mixed offenders. Participants' static and dynamic risk factors and risks of sexual reoffending, as well as their offense records and motivations, were measured and analyzed. Results supported the self-regulation model. Each offender type was related to different levels of static and dynamic risk factors and to different pathway. For example, incest offenders represented the avoidant-passive pathway while rapists represented approach-automatic pathway, with impulsivity and general criminality. The approach-automatic pathway was equally comprised of rapists, child molesters, and incest offenders. This implies that different offenders have different motivations and internal and external processes to offending behaviors. Implications of the findings are discussed.

Keywords: self-regulation model, rapist, child molester, sexual offender

98. Yoder, J. R., Hansen, J., Lobanov-Rostovsky, C., & Ruch, D. (2015). The impact of family service involvement on treatment completion and general recidivism among male youthful sexual offenders. *Journal of Offender Rehabilitation, 54*(4), 256-277. http://dx.doi.org/10.1080/10509674.2015.1025177

The fields of intervention programs for adolescent sex offenders have moved toward family- and community-oriented services, yet the programs still suffer from lack of empirical support for their effectiveness. To evaluate the outcomes of family service, the present article investigates the effect of involvement in family service on treatment completion and recidivism rates in male adolescent sex offenders through a review of data files. Six types of family-oriented practices were included in the review: family therapy, multifamily group therapy, caregiver in the multidisciplinary team (MDT), family member in MDT, informed supervision, and family reunification. The analyses showed that youth who were involved in greater family service or were placed in home had higher treatment completion rates. However, their relationships with recidivism rate were not found to be significant. These findings might provide support for the roles of family as a protective factor for recidivism in adolescent offenders.

Implications for future treatment programs and policies are discussed.

Keywords: psychopathology, adolescent sex offender, family service, treatment

99. Young, B. J., & Furman, W. (2013). Predicting commitment in young adults' physically aggressive and sexually coercive dating relationships. *Journal of Interpersonal Violence, 28*(17), 3245-3264. http://dx.doi.org/10.1177/0886260513496897

Although violent dating relationships which accompany physical aggression or sexual coercion often cause significant mental distress in young women, some individuals still decide to continue the relationships. The present article investigates predictors of emerging adults' engagement in physically aggressive or sexually coercive dating relationship using Rusbult's Investment Model of romantic relationship. Data from 148 female college students who completed the 6-month longitudinal assessments were collected. The participants' experience of physical aggression and sexual coercion in the relationships, relationship investment, rejection sensitivity, romantic relationship styles, and relationship outcomes were assessed and analyzed. The results showed that women who discontinued the relationship experienced lower relationship satisfaction, lower investment, lower relationship commitment, and higher perceived quality of alternative relationships. Low relationship commitment and high rejection sensitivity was related to dissolution of relationship after six months. Rejection sensitivity and anxious attachment styles were strongly correlated, and an avoidant style was indirectly related to commitment through satisfaction, investment, and perceived quality of alternatives. The findings add to the knowledge about mechanisms of relationship commitment, which might be helpful to guide future interventions to empower women in violent relationships.

Keywords: school-based concerns, dating violence, relationship, rejection sensitivity, relationship commitment

100. Zweig, J. M., Dank, M., Yahner, J., & Lachman, P. (2013). The rate of cyber dating abuse among teens and how it relates to other forms of teen dating violence. *Journal of Youth and Adolescence, 42*(7), 1063-1077. http://dx.doi.org/10.1007/s10964-013-9922-8

The present article explores the prevalence of cyber dating abuse in adolescents and its relationship with other forms of dating violence (e.g. sexual coercion, emotional aggression, and physical violence). A total of 3,745 adolescents reported currently being in a relationship or having been in a relationship in the previous year. About 26% of participants in a current or recent relationship reported victimization from cyber dating violence. Two forms of sexual cyber dating violence were also reported from a total of 14% of the participants. Female students reported more victimization from cyber dating violence than male students, especially sexual cyber dating violence. The risks of experiencing sexual coercion were seven times higher for victims of sexual cyber than non-victims. About 10% of the participants reported perpetration of some form of cyber dating violence. Female students reported more perpetration of non-sexual cyber dating violence while male students reported more perpetration of sexual cyber dating violence. The risks of perpetration of sexual coercion were 20 times higher for perpetrators of sexual cyber dating violence than non-perpetrators. Reports of victimization experience among perpetrators were not uncommon in the sample. Implications of the findings for prevention programs and for future research are described.

Keywords: technology-involved issues, cyber dating violence, sexual coercion, adolescent dating violence

# References

Aberle, C. C., & Littlefield, R. P. (2001). Family functioning and sexual aggression in a sample of college men. *Journal of Interpersonal Violence, 16*(6), 565-579. http://dx.doi.org/10.1177/088626001016006005

Acierno, R., Brady, K., Gray, M., Kilpatrick, D. G., Resnick, H., & Best, C. L. (2002). Psychopathology following interpersonal violence: A comparison of risk factors in older and younger adults. *Journal of Clinical Geropsychology, 8*(1), 13-23. http://dx.doi.org/10.1023/A:1013041907018

Acierno, R., Resnick, H. S., Flood, A., & Holmes, M. (2003). An acute post-rape intervention to prevent substance use and abuse. *Addictive Behaviors, 28*(9), 1701-1715. http://dx.doi.org/10.1016/j.addbeh.2003.08.043

Ackard, D. M., & Neumark-Sztainer, D. (2002). Date violence and date rape among adolescents: Associations with disordered eating behaviors and psychological health. *Child Abuse & Neglect, 26*(5), 455-473. http://dx.doi.org/10.1016/S0145-2134(02)00322-8

Alink, L. R. A., Euser, S., Bakermans-Kranenburg, M. J., & van IJzendoorn, M. H. (2014). A challenging job: Physical and sexual violence towards group workers in youth residential care. *Child & Youth Care Forum, 43*(2), 243-250. http://dx.doi.org/10.1007/s10566-013-9236-8

Allroggen, M., Rau, T., Ohlert, J., & Fegert, J. M. (2017). Lifetime prevalence and incidence of sexual

victimization of adolescents in institutional care. *Child Abuse & Neglect, 66*, 23-30.
http://dx.doi.org/10.1016/j.chiabu.2017.02.015

Angelone, D. J., Mitchell, D., & Grossi, L. (2015). Men's perceptions of an acquaintance rape: The role of relationship length, victim resistance, and gender role attitudes. *Journal of Interpersonal Violence, 30*(13), 2278-2303.
http://dx.doi.org/10.1177/0886260514552448

Arata, C. M., & Lindman, L. (2002). Marriage, child abuse, and sexual revictimization. *Journal of Interpersonal Violence, 17*(9), 953-971.
http://dx.doi.org/10.1177/0886260502017009003

Ashmore, T., Spangaro, J., & McNamara, L. (2015). 'I was raped by Santa Claus': Responding to disclosures of sexual assault in mental health inpatient facilities. *International Journal of Mental Health Nursing, 24*(2), 139-148.
http://dx.doi.org/10.1111/inm.12114

Baker, M. W., Sugar, N. F., & Eckert, L. O. (2009). Sexual assault of older women: Risk and vulnerability by living arrangement. *Sexuality Research & Social Policy: A Journal of the NSRC, 6*(4), 79-87.
http://dx.doi.org/10.1525/srsp.2009.6.4.79

Bindesbøl Holm Johansen, K., Pedersen, B. M., & Tjørnhøj-Thomsen, T. (2018). Visual gossiping: Non-consensual 'nude' sharing among young people in Denmark. *Culture, Health & Sexuality*. Advance online publication.
http://dx.doi.org/10.1080/13691058.2018.1534140

Brown, S. L., & Forth, A. E. (1997). Psychopathy and sexual assault: Static risk factors, emotional precursors, and rapist subtypes. *Journal of Consulting and Clinical Psychology, 65*(5), 848-857.

Burgess, A. W., & Morgenbesser, L. I. (2005). Sexual violence and seniors. *Brief Treatment and Crisis Intervention, 5*(2), 193-202.
http://dx.doi.org/10.1093/brief-treatment/mhi016

Caron, S. L., & Carter, D. B. (1997). The relationships among sex role orientation, egalitarianism, attitudes toward sexuality, and attitudes toward violence against women. The *Journal of Social Psychology, 137*(5), 568-587.
http://dx.doi.org/10.1080/00224549709595479

Carr, J. L., & VanDeusen, K. M. (2002). The relationship between family of origin violence and dating violence in college men. *Journal of Interpersonal Violence, 17*(6), 630-646
http://dx.doi.org/10.1177/0886260502017006003

Casey, E. A., Leek, C., Tolman, R. M., Allen, C. T., & Carlson, J. M. (2017). Getting men in the room: Perceptions of effective strategies to initiate men's involvement in gender-based violence prevention in a global sample. *Culture, Health & Sexuality, 19*(9), 979-995.
http://dx.doi.org/10.1080/13691058.2017.1281438

Casey, E. A., Tolman, R. M., Carlson, J., Allen, C. sT., & Storer, H. L. (2017). What motivates men's involvement in gender-based violence prevention? Latent class profiles and correlates in an international sample of men. *Men and Masculinities, 20*(3), 294-316.

Ceccato, V. (2014). The nature of rape places. *Journal of Environmental Psychology, 40*, 97-107. http://dx.doi.org/10.1016/j.jenvp.2014.05.006

Chan, K. L. (2011). Correlates of childhood sexual abuse and intimate partner sexual victimization. *Partner Abuse, 2*(3), 365-381. http://dx.doi.org/10.1891/1946-6560.2.3.365

Cohen, L. J., & Galynker, I. I. (2002). Clinical features of pedophilia and implications for treatment. *Journal of Psychiatric Practice, 8*(5), 276-289. http://dx.doi.org/10.1097/00131746-200209000-00004

Craig, L. A., Browne, K. D., Beech, A., & Stringer, I. (2006). Differences in personality and risk characteristics in sex, violent and general offenders. *Criminal Behaviour and Mental Health, 16*(3), 183-194. http://dx.doi.org/10.1002/cbm.618

Crockett, C., Cooper, B., & Brandl, B. (2018). Intersectional stigma and late-life intimate-partner and sexual violence: How social workers can bolster safety and healing for older survivors. *British Journal of Social Work, 48*(4), 1000-1013. http://dx.doi.org/10.1093/bjsw/bcy049

Daigneault, I., Vézina-Gagnon, P., Bourgeois, C., Esposito, T., & Hébert, M. (2017). Physical and mental health of children with substantiated sexual abuse: Gender comparisons from a matched-control cohort study. *Child Abuse & Neglect, 66*, 155-165. http://dx.doi.org/10.1016/j.chiabu.2017.02.038

Del Bove, G., Stermac, L., & Bainbridge, D. (2005). Comparisons of sexual assault among older and younger women. *Journal of Elder Abuse & Neglect, 17*(3), 1-18. http://dx.doi.org/10.1300/J084v17n03_01

Dellazizzo, L., Dugré, J. R., Berwald, M., Stafford, M.-C., Côté, G., Potvin, S., & Dumais, A. (2018). Distinct pathological profiles of inmates showcasing cluster B personality traits, mental disorders and substance use regarding violent behaviors. *Psychiatry Research, 260,* 371-378.
http://dx.doi.org/10.1016/j.psychres.2017.12.006

Diehl, C., Rees, J., & Bohner, G. (2018). Predicting sexual harassment from hostile sexism and short-term mating orientation: Relative strength of predictors depends on situational priming of power versus sex. *Violence Against Women, 24*(2), 123-143.
http://dx.doi.org/10.1177/1077801216678092

Draucker, C., & Martsolf, D. (2010). Life-course typology of adults who experienced sexual violence. *Journal of Interpersonal Violence, 25*(7), 1155-1182.
http://dx.doi.org/10.1177/0886260509340537

Draucker, C. B., Martsolf, D. S., Roller, C., Knapik, G. P., Ross, R., & Stidham, A. W. (2011). Healing from childhood sexual abuse: A theoretical model. *Journal of Child Sexual Abuse: Research, Treatment, & Program Innovations for Victims, Survivors, & Offenders, 20*(4), 435-466.
http://dx.doi.org/10.1080/10538712.2011.588188

Drouin, M., Ross, J., & Tobin, E. (2015). Sexting: A new, digital vehicle for intimate partner aggression? *Computers in Human Behavior, 50,* 197-204.
http://dx.doi.org/10.1016/j.chb.2015.04.001

Dworkin, E. R., Menon, S. V., Bystrynski, J., & Allen, N. E. (2017). Sexual assault victimization and psychopathology: A review and meta-analysis.

*Clinical Psychology Review, 56*, 65-81.
http://dx.doi.org/10.1016/j.cpr.2017.06.002

Epstein, M. H. (2004). Behavioral and Emotional Rating Scale: A strength-based approach to assessment (Examiner's manual) (2nd ed.). Austin, TX: Pro-Ed.

Eyssel, F., & Bohner, G. (2011). Schema effects of rape myth acceptance on judgments of guilt and blame in rape cases: The role of perceived entitlement to judge. *Journal of Interpersonal Violence, 26*(8), 1579-1605.
http://dx.doi.org/10.1177/0886260510370593

Feiring, C., Simon, V. A., Cleland, C. M., & Barrett, E. P. (2013). Potential pathways from stigmatization and externalizing behavior to anger and dating aggression in sexually abused youth. *Journal of Clinical Child and Adolescent Psychology, 42*(3), 309-322.
http://dx.doi.org/10.1080/15374416.2012.736083

Foa, E. B., Hearst-Ikeda, D., & Perry, K. J. (1995). Evaluation of a brief cognitive-behavioral program for the prevention of chronic PTSD in recent assault victims. *Journal of Consulting and Clinical Psychology, 63*(6), 948-955.
http://dx.doi.org/10.1016/j.addbeh.2003.08.043

Foshee, V. A., Bauman, K. E., Ennett, S. T., Suchindran, C., Benefield, T., & Linder, G. F. (2005). Assessing the effects of the dating violence prevention program "Safe Dates" using random coefficient regression modeling. *Prevention Science, 6*(3), 245-258. http://dx.doi.org/10.1007/s11121-005-0007-0

Foshee, V. A., Benefield, T. S., Ennett, S. T., Bauman, K. E., & Suchindran, C. (2004). Longitudinal predictors of serious physical and sexual dating violence victimization during adolescence. *Preventive Medicine: An International Journal Devoted to Practice and Theory, 39*(5), 1007-1016. http://dx.doi.org/10.1016/j.ypmed.2004.04.014

Gannon, T. A., Collie, R. M., Ward, T., & Thakker, J. (2008). Rape: Psychopathology, theory and treatment. *Clinical Psychology Review, 28*(6), 982-1008. http://dx.doi.org/10.1016/j.cpr.2008.02.005

Gartner, R. E., & Sterzing, P. R. (2016). Gender microaggressions as a gateway to sexual harassment and sexual assault: Expanding the conceptualization of youth sexual violence. Affilia: *Journal of Women & Social Work, 31*(4), 491-503. http://dx.doi.org/10.1177/0886109916654732

Gokten, E. S., & Duman, N. S. (2016). Factors influencing the development of psychiatric disorders in the victims of sexual abuse: A study on Turkish children. *Children and Youth Services Review, 69*, 49-55. http://dx.doi.org/10.1016/j.childyouth.2016.07.022

Grove, L., Morrison-Beedy, D., Kirby, R., & Hess, J. (2018). The birds, bees, and special needs: Making evidence-based sex education accessible for adolescents with intellectual disabilities. *Sexuality and Disability*. Advance online publication.

Hald, G. M., Malamuth, N. M., & Yuen, C. (2010). Pornography and attitudes supporting violence against women: revisiting the relationship in nonexperimental studies. *Aggressive Behavior, 36*(1), 14-20. https://doi.org/10.1002/ab.20328

Hare, R. D. (2003). *Hare PCL-R* (2nd ed.). New York, NY: Multi-Health Systems.

Harvey, M. (1993, June). *Traumatic memory research and practice*. Paper presented at the "Memories of Abuse" conference, Minneapolis, MN.

Hayes, R. M., & Dragiewicz, M. (2018). Unsolicited dick pics: Erotica, exhibitionism or entitlement? *Women's Studies International Forum*. Advance online publication. http://dx.doi.org/10.1016/j.wsif.2018.07.001

Hedge, J. M., Sianko, N., & McDonell, J. R. (2017). Professional help-seeking for adolescent dating violence in the rural south: The role of social support and informal help-seeking. *Violence Against Women*, *23*(12), 1442-1461. http://dx.doi.org/10.1177/1077801216662342

Henry, N., & Powell, A. (2015). Embodied harms: Gender, shame, and technology-facilitated sexual violence. *Violence Against Women*, *21*(6), 758-779. http://dx.doi.org/10.1177/1077801215576581

Herman, J. (1992). *Trauma and recovery*. New York: HarperCollins.

Hillenbrand-Gunn, T. L., Heppner, M. J., Mauch, P. A., & Park, H.-J. (2010). Men as Allies: The efficacy of a high school rape prevention intervention. *Journal of Counseling & Development*, *88*(1), 43-51. http://dx.doi.org/10.1002/j.1556-6678.2010.tb00149.x

Hunter, J. A. (1991). A comparison of the psychosocial maladjustment of adult males and females sexually molested as children. *Journal of*

*Interpersonal Violence, 6*(2), 205-217.
http://dx.doi.org/10.1177/088626091006002005

Jackson, S. M., Cram, F., & Seymour, F. W. (2000).
Violence and sexual coercion in high school students'
dating relationships. *Journal of Family Violence, 15*(1),
23-36. http://dx.doi.org/10.1023/A:1007545302987

Jeary, K. (2005). Sexual abuse and sexual offending
against elderly people: A focus on perpetrators and
victims. *Journal of Forensic Psychiatry & Psychology,
16*(2), 328-343.
http://dx.doi.org/10.1080/14789940500096115

Kloess, J. A., Beech, A. R., & Harkins, L. (2014).
Online child sexual exploitation: Prevalence, process,
and offender characteristics. *Trauma, Violence, &
Abuse, 15*(2), 126-139.
http://dx.doi.org/10.1177/1524838013511543

Knight, L., & Hester, M. (2016). Domestic violence
and mental health in older adults. *International
Review of Psychiatry, 28*(5), 464–474.
https://doi.org/10.1080/09540261.2016.1215294

Kosson, D. S., Kelly, J. C., & White, J. W. (1997).
Psychopathy-related traits predict self-reported sexual
aggression among college men. *Journal of
Interpersonal Violence, 12*(2), 241-254.
http://dx.doi.org/10.1177/088626097012002006

Krahé, B., Berger, A., Vanwesenbeeck, I., Bianchi, G.,
Chliaoutakis, J., Fernández-Fuertes, A. A., . . .
Zygadło, A. (2015). Prevalence and correlates of
young people's sexual aggression perpetration and
victimisation in 10 European countries: A multi-level
analysis. *Culture, Health & Sexuality, 17*(6), 682-699.
http://dx.doi.org/10.1080/13691058.2014.989265

Langhinrichsen-Rohling, J., & Rohling, M. (2000). Negative family-of-origin experiences: Are they associated with perpetrating unwanted pursuit behaviors? *Violence and Victims, 15*(4), 459-471.

Lebowitz, L., Harvey, M. R., & Herman, J. L. (1993). A stage-by-dimension model of recovery from sexual trauma. *Journal of Interpersonal Violence, 8*(3), 378-391. http://dx.doi.org/10.1177/088626093008003006

Levenson, J. S., & Socia, K. M. (2016). Adverse childhood experiences and arrest patterns in a sample of sexual offenders. *Journal of Interpersonal Violence, 31*(10), 1883-1911. http://dx.doi.org/10.1177/0886260515570751

Levine, E. (2017). Sexual violence among middle school students: The effects of gender and dating experience. *Journal of Interpersonal Violence, 32*(14), 2059-2082. http://dx.doi.org/10.1177/0886260515590786

McCloskey, L. A. (2013). The intergenerational transfer of mother–daughter risk for gender-based abuse. *Psychodynamic Psychiatry, 41*(2), 303-328. http://dx.doi.org/10.1521/pdps.2013.41.2.303

McQuiller Williams, L., Porter, J. L., & Smith, T. R. (2016). Understanding date rape attitudes and behaviors: Exploring the influence of race, gender, and prior sexual victimization. *Victims & Offenders, 11*(2), 173-198. http://dx.doi.org/10.1080/15564886.2014.960025

Mercado, C. C., & Ogloff, J. R. P. (2007). Risk and the preventive detention of sex offenders in Australia and the United States. *International Journal of Law*

and Psychiatry, 30(1), 49-59.
http://dx.doi.org/10.1016/j.ijlp.2006.02.001

Morgan, W., & Gilchrist, E. (2010). Risk assessment with intimate partner sex offenders. Journal of Sexual Aggression, 16(3), 361-372.
http://dx.doi.org/10.1080/13552600.2010.502976

Nason, E. E., & Yeater, E. A. (2012). Sexual attitudes mediate the relationship between sexual victimization history and women's response effectiveness. Journal of Interpersonal Violence, 27(13), 2565-2581.
http://dx.doi.org/10.1177/0886260512436393

Ngo, Q. M., Veliz, P. T., Kusunoki, Y., Stein, S. F., & Boyd, C. J. (2018). Adolescent sexual violence: Prevalence, adolescent risks, and violence characteristics. Preventive Medicine: An International Journal Devoted to Practice and Theory, 116, 68-74.
http://dx.doi.org/10.1016/j.ypmed.2018.08.032

Nichols, K. (2018). Moving beyond ideas of laddism: Conceptualising 'mischievous masculinities' as a new way of understanding everyday sexism and gender relations. Journal of Gender Studies, 27(1), 73-85.
http://dx.doi.org/10.1080/09589236.2016.1202815

Novack, S. (2017). Sex ed in higher ed: Should we say yes to "affirmative consent"? Studies in Gender and Sexuality, 18(4), 302-312.
http://dx.doi.org/10.1080/15240657.2017.1383074

Ohlert, J., Seidler, C., Rau, T., Fegert, J., & Allroggen, M. (2017). Comparison of psychopathological symptoms in adolescents who experienced sexual violence as a victim and/or as a perpetrator. Journal of Child Sexual Abuse: Research, Treatment, & Program Innovations for Victims, Survivors, &

*Offenders, 26*(4), 373-387.
http://dx.doi.org/10.1080/10538712.2017.1283652

Pashang, S., Khanlou, N., & Clarke, J. (2018). The mental health impact of cyber sexual violence on youth identity. *International Journal of Mental Health and Addiction*. Advance online publication. http://dx.doi.org/10.1007/s11469-018-0032-4

Piccigallo, J. R., Lilley, T. G., & Miller, S. L. (2012). "it's cool to care about sexual violence": Men's experiences with sexual assault prevention. *Men and Masculinities, 15*(5), 507-525. http://dx.doi.org/10.1177/1097184X12458590

Pina, A., Holland, J., & James, M. (2017). The malevolent side of revenge porn proclivity: Dark personality traits and sexist ideology. *International Journal of Technoethics, 8*(1), 30-43. http://dx.doi.org/10.4018/IJT.2017010103

Polaschek, D. L. L., Ward, T., & Hudson, S. M. (1997). Rape and rapists: Theory and treatment. *Clinical Psychology Review, 17*(2), 117-144. http://dx.doi.org/10.1016/S0272-7358(96)00048-7

Pryor, D. W., & Hughes, M. R. (2013). Fear of rape among college women: A social psychological analysis. *Violence and Victims, 28*(3), 443-465. http://dx.doi.org/10.1891/0886-6708.VV-D-12-00029

Quinsey, V. L., Harris, G. T., Rice, M. E., & Cormier, C. A. (2006).*Violent offenders: Appraising and managing risk* (2nd ed.). Washington, DC: American Psychological Association.

Ramsey-Klawsnik, H. (2003). Elder sexual abuse within the family. *Journal of Elder Abuse & Neglect,*

*15*(1), 43-58.
http://dx.doi.org/10.1300/J084v15n01_04

Rebocho, M. F., & Gonçalves, R. A. (2012). Sexual predators and prey: A comparative study of the hunting behavior of rapists and child molesters. *Journal of Interpersonal Violence, 27*(14), 2770-2789. http://dx.doi.org/10.1177/0886260512438280

Rice, M. E., & Harris, G. T. (2014). What does it mean when age is related to recidivism among sex offenders? *Law and Human Behavior, 38*(2), 151-161. http://dx.doi.org/10.1037/lhb0000052

Richardson, E. W., Simons, L. G., & Futris, T. G. (2017). Linking family-of-origin experiences and perpetration of sexual coercion: College males' sense of entitlement. *Journal of Child and Family Studies, 26*(3), 781-791. http://dx.doi.org/10.1007/s10826-016-0592-5

Roberts, A. L., Koenen, K. C., Lyall, K., Robinson, E. B., & Weisskopf, M. G. (2015). Association of autistic traits in adulthood with childhood abuse, interpersonal victimization, and posttraumatic stress. *Child Abuse & Neglect, 45*, 135-142. http://dx.doi.org/10.1016/j.chiabu.2015.04.010

Rodgers, K. B., & Hust, S. J. T. (2018). Sexual objectification in music videos and acceptance of potentially offensive sexual behaviors. *Psychology of Popular Media Culture, 7*(4), 413-428. http://dx.doi.org/10.1037/ppm0000142

Romero-Sánchez, M., Carretero-Dios, H., Megías, J. L., Moya, M., & Ford, T. E. (2017). Sexist humor and rape proclivity: The moderating role of joke teller gender and severity of sexual assault. *Violence*

*Against Women, 23*(8), 951-972.
http://dx.doi.org/10.1177/1077801216654017

Scarpati, A. S., & Pina, A. (2017). Cultural and moral dimensions of sexual aggression: The role of moral disengagement in men's likelihood to sexually aggress. *Aggression and Violent Behavior, 37*, 115-121. http://dx.doi.org/10.1016/j.avb.2017.09.001

Schwark, S. (2017). Visual representations of sexual violence in online news outlets. *Frontiers in Psychology, 8*, Article ID 774.

Seto, M. C., & Lalumière, M. L. (2010). What is so special about male adolescent sexual offending? A review and test of explanations through meta-analysis. *Psychological Bulletin, 136*(4), 526-575. http://dx.doi.org/10.1037/a0019700

Silva, T., Woodhams, J., & Harkins, L. (2017). "An adventure that went wrong": Reasons given by convicted perpetrators of multiple perpetrator sexual offending for their involvement in the offense. *Archives of Sexual Behavior.* Advance online publication. http://dx.doi.org/10.1007/s10508-017-1011-8

Simons, L. G., Burt, C. H., & Simons, R. L. (2008). A test of explanations for the effect of harsh parenting on the perpetration of dating violence and sexual coercion among college males. *Violence and Victims, 23*(1), 66-82. http://dx.doi.org/10.1891/0886-6708.23.1.66

Simons, L. G., Simons, R. L., Lei, M.-K., & Sutton, T. E. (2012). Exposure to harsh parenting and pornography as explanations for males' sexual coercion and females' sexual victimization. *Violence*

and Victims, 27(3), 378-395.
http://dx.doi.org/10.1891/0886-6708.27.3.378

Soylu, N., Ayaz, M., Gökten, E. S., Alpaslan, A. H., Dönmez, Y. E., Özcan, Ö. Ö., . . . Tufan, A. E. (2016). Gender differences in sexually abused children and adolescents: A multicenter study in Turkey. Journal of Child Sexual Abuse: Research, Treatment, & Program Innovations for Victims, Survivors, & Offenders, 25(4), 415-427.
http://dx.doi.org/10.1080/10538712.2016.1143073

Starfelt, L. C., Young, R. M., White, K. M., & Palk, G. R. M. (2015). Explicating the role of sexual coercion and vulnerability alcohol expectancies in rape attributions. Journal of Interpersonal Violence, 30(11), 1965-1981.
http://dx.doi.org/10.1177/0886260514549466

Süssenbach, P., Eyssel, F., Rees, J., & Bohner, G. (2017). Looking for blame: Rape myth acceptance and attention to victim and perpetrator. Journal of Interpersonal Violence, 32(15), 2323-2344.
http://dx.doi.org/10.1177/0886260515591975

Sutton, T. E., & Simons, L. G. (2015). Sexual assault among college students: Family of origin hostility, attachment, and the hook-up culture as risk factors. Journal of Child and Family Studies, 24(10), 2827-2840. http://dx.doi.org/10.1007/s10826-014-0087-1

Totten, M. (2003). Girlfriend abuse as a form of masculinity construction among violent, marginal male youth. Men and Masculinities, 6(1), 70-92.
http://dx.doi.org/10.1177/1097184X03253138

Turchik, J. A., Hebenstreit, C. L., & Judson, S. S. (2016). An examination of the gender inclusiveness of current theories of sexual violence in adulthood: Recognizing male victims, female perpetrators, and same-sex violence. *Trauma, Violence, & Abuse, 17*(2), 133-148. http://dx.doi.org/10.1177/1524838014566721

Van Bruggen, L. K., Runtz, M. G., & Kadlec, H. (2006). Sexual Revictimization: The role of sexual self-esteem and dysfunctional sexual behaviors. *Child Maltreatment, 11*(2), 131-145. http://dx.doi.org/10.1177/1077559505285780

Van Ness, S. R. (1984). Rape as instrumental violence: A study of youth offenders. *Journal of Offender Counseling, Services & Rehabilitation, 9*(1-2), 161-170. http://dx.doi.org/10.1300/J264v09n01_11

Veneziano, C., & Veneziano, L. (2002). Adolescent sex offenders: A review of the literature. *Trauma, Violence, & Abuse, 3*(4), 247-260. https://doi.org/10.1177/1524838002237329

Vonderhaar, R. L., & Carmody, D. C. (2015). There are no "innocent victims": The influence of just world beliefs and prior victimization on rape myth acceptance. *Journal of Interpersonal Violence, 30*(10), 1615-1632. http://dx.doi.org/10.1177/0886260514549196

Ward, T., & Hudson, S. M. (1998). A model of the relapse process in sexual offenders. *Journal of Interpersonal Violence, 13*, 700–725.

Weare, S. (2018). From coercion to physical force: Aggressive strategies used by women against men in "forced-to-penetrate" cases in the uk. *Archives of Sexual Behavior. 47*(8), 2191-2205. http://dx.doi.org/10.1007/s10508-018-1232-5

Weiler, J. V. (2015). Living in the era of digital exhibitionism. *Child & Youth Services, 36*(4), 329-344. http://dx.doi.org/10.1080/0145935X.2015.1096596

Worling, J. R. (2004). The Estimate of Risk of Adolescent Sexual Offense Recidivism (ERASOR): Preliminary psychometric data. *Sexual Abuse: A Journal of Research & Treatment, 16*(3), 235–254.

Worling, J. R., & Langton, C. M. (2012). Assessment and treatment of adolescents who sexually offend: Clinical issues and implications for secure settings. *Criminal Justice and Behavior, 39*(6), 814-841. http://dx.doi.org/10.1177/0093854812439378

Worling, J. R., & Langton, C. M. (2015). A prospective investigation of factors that predict desistance from recidivism for adolescents who have sexually offended. *Sexual Abuse: Journal of Research and Treatment, 27*(1), 127-142. http://dx.doi.org/10.1177/1079063214549260

Yates, P. M., & Kingston, D. A. (2006). The self-regulation model of sexual offending: The relationship between offence pathways and static and dynamic sexual offence risk. *Sexual Abuse: Journal of Research and Treatment, 18*(3), 259-270. http://dx.doi.org/10.1177/107906320601800304

Yoder, J. R., Hansen, J., Lobanov-Rostovsky, C., & Ruch, D. (2015). The impact of family service involvement on treatment completion and general recidivism among male youthful sexual offenders. *Journal of Offender Rehabilitation, 54*(4), 256-277. http://dx.doi.org/10.1080/10509674.2015.1025177

Young, B. J., & Furman, W. (2013). Predicting commitment in young adults' physically aggressive and sexually coercive dating relationships. *Journal of Interpersonal Violence, 28*(17), 3245-3264. http://dx.doi.org/10.1177/0886260513496897

Zweig, J. M., Dank, M., Yahner, J., & Lachman, P. (2013). The rate of cyber dating abuse among teens and how it relates to other forms of teen dating violence. *Journal of Youth and Adolescence, 42*(7), 1063-1077. http://dx.doi.org/10.1007/s

# Index

Note: Numbering refers to the bibliography entry, not to a page number. This is to accommodate e-readers, which often repaginate the content.

exposures, early, 15, 79

Exposure to harsh parenting and pornography, 82

externalizing, 32

F

family, 1, 8, 15, 19, 42, 52, 54, 56, 60, 70, 73, 81–82, 86, 89, 95–96, 98

  traditional, 87

family environments, 1

family members, 13, 16, 54, 70, 83, 93, 98

  incarcerated, 54

family-of-origin, 15, 81

family-of-origin experience, 52

  negative, 52, 86, 91

family-of-origin factors, 1, 8, 73, 82, 86

family-of-origin histories, 45

family-oriented practices, 98

family problems, 54, 79

family reunification, 98

family service, 98

family service involvement, 98

family therapy, 98

functions, cognitive, 13, 36, 91

T

# About Minnesota Center for Nonviolence

Minnesota Center for Nonviolence (MCNV) is a nonprofit founded in 2012. Its mission is to help individuals and communities develop the resources and skills needed to live nonviolently in a complex world.

MCNV core operating principles can be summed up as:

Apolitical

Collective

Autonomous

Grass roots

Project based

Supportive

If you would like more information about MCNV, please visit minnesotacenterfornonviolence.org.

# Author information

E. J. Cho is a graduate student in Social Work. Her professional interests include clinical psychology, counseling and social work.

Leonard Snyder is a psychotherapist and college professor. He has over twenty years of experience in higher education. He is the founder of the Minnesota Center for Nonviolence. Leonard has worked for over a decade with victim/survivors and perpetrators of intimate partner and sexual violence.

Herbert H. Laube is a marriage and family therapist, college professor, and life management and planning consultant. Herb has many years of scholarship in family and sexual relationship counseling and sexual behavior. He has held faculty positions at several universities and graduate schools.